HOW WOMEN CAN ADVANCE IN BUSINESS

And Break the Glass Ceiling

ROBERTA CAVA

How Women Can Advance in Business

And Break the Glass Ceiling

Roberta Cava

Published by Cava Consulting

105 / 3 Township Drive,

Burleigh Heads, 4220, Queensland, Australia

info@dealingwithdifficultpeople.info

Discover other titles by Roberta Cava at
www.dealingwithdifficultpeople.info

National Library of Australia

Cataloguing-in-publication data:

ISBN 978-0-9923402-3-0

BOOKS BY ROBERTA CAVA

Dealing with Difficult People

(22 publishers – in 16 languages)

Dealing with Difficult Situations – at Work and at Home

Dealing with Difficult Spouses and Children

Dealing with Difficult Relatives and In-Laws

Dealing with Domestic Violence and Child Abuse

Dealing with School Bullying

Dealing with Workplace Bullying

What am I going to do with the rest of my life?

Before tying the knot – Questions couples Must ask each other

Before they marry!

How Women can advance in business

Survival Skills for Supervisors and Managers

Human Resources at its Best!

Human Resources Policies and Procedures

Employee Handbooks

Easy Come – Hard to go – The Art of Hiring, Disciplining and
Firing Employees

Time and Stress – Today's silent killers

Take Command of your Future – Make things Happen

Belly Laughs for All! – Volumes 1 – 4

Wisdom of the World! The happy, sad and wise things in life!

ACKNOWLEDGEMENTS

Without the help of four distinct groups, this book would not have been possible:

1. Over 700 managers who identified why they weren't promoting more women;

2. The hundreds of women who took time to explain the difficulties they were running into as they tried to escape from their pink-collar ghetto positions.

3. The women who attended my *Escaping the Pink-Collar Ghetto, Cracking the Glass Ceiling* and *The Balancing Act* seminars who gave me more insight into the home and work problems women were facing.

4. Those women who had achieved success and were willing to explain the steps they'd taken to succeed.

Special thanks to Patti Connolly, who edited the original edition of this book and Victoria Heron who edited the eBook edition.

DEDICATION

Dedicated to my male and female friends who have kept me up-to-date with new developments for women in business and to the participants of my seminars who have kindly passed on their ideas so that others might benefit from their experiences.

HOW WOMEN CAN
ADVANCE IN BUSINESS

Table of Contents

- Where do you fit
  - stay-at-home moms
  - family as first priority but must work
  - career as first priority
- Childcare
- How can you obtain your family's help at home
  - family conferences
  - husband objects to wife working
  - overcoming objections
- Giving loving time to your family
- Husband's quality time
- Equality
- Introducing business to home management
- Which career choice is best for you?

- Barriers to promotion
- No career goals
- Overtime, travelling on business,
- Re-location
- Attendance problems
- Super-woman
- Personal problems taken to work
- Gossip
- Afraid of confrontation
- Low self-esteem
- Poor communicators
- Can't take rejection of ideas

- Using 'female tricks'
- Women sabotaging other women
- Poor decision-makers
- Men protecting women
- Require more training
- Promoted without training
- Don't know what they're supposed to do
- Women not using 'unique' talents
- Are 'women libbers'

- Never undermine boss
- Do your own job
- Must show respect to boss
- Double-check when offered a promotion
- Accepting too many responsibilities
- Know company hierarchy
- Line and Staff positions
- Diversification of experience
- Careless work habits
- Supervisory line-of-command
- Military tactics
- Team sports in the workplace
- Conform to rules of the game
- Use of female strengths
- Dating co-workers
- Boss taking credit for your work
- Using logic instead of emotion

- Career planning
- What is a job, an occupation and a career?
- Mid-life career changes
- The importance of setting career goals
- Determining your transferrable skills
- Career changes
- Freedom from the pink-collar ghetto

- Choosing a professional career counsellor
- Tests and tools
- Career planning information
- Goal setting problems
- Goal setting plan
- Guidelines for setting career goals
- How I obtained career counselling

- Equal pay for work of equal value
- Part-time workers
- Selling yourself in an interview
- Interview tips
- Discrimination and Human Rights
- Application forms
- What can and cannot be asked on application forms and at interviews
- Questions women are often asked on interviews
- Tricky interview questions
- How to obtain the salary you're worth
- Written job offers
- Less work - more pay
- Asking for a raise

- How to handle being overlooked for a promotion
- Acting positions
- Work related problems
- The 'leap-frog' syndrome
- The dead-end job
- Foot-dragging co-workers
- Dumping or 'job enlargement'
- Overtime – overload
- Understaffed
- The disorganised boss
- Too many bosses

- Job classification inequities
- You're now a supervisor!

- Being a female boss
- Uncooperative staff
- Supervising older workers
- Supervising men
- Supervising former peers
- Boss disciplines in public
- Aggressive female label
- Invades privacy
- The importance of obtaining supervisory training

- Essential supervisory responsibilities
- The role of the supervisor
- Leadership styles
- The delegation process
- Meeting skills
- Motivation
- Time management
- Problem solving and decision-making
- Interpersonal skills
- Employment interviewing
- Training and development
- Employee discipline
- Socialising with staff
- Supervisory problems

- Behaviour styles
- Consequences of using the 3 major behaviour styles
- Manipulation
- Confidence in speaking
- Self-sabotage
- Fear of success/failure

- Handling guilt
- Learning how to take risks
- Accepting compliments
- How to increase self-esteem
- How to let people know you're a positive thinker
- Support groups
- Self-image
- How to dress for success

- Why are some men intimidated by assertive women?
- How to deal with male chauvinism
- Sexual harassment
- How to handle sexual harassment

- Rules for female rookies
- Tips for female travellers
- Travel safety tips
- Fire safety
- Women travellers' rooms

- Networking
- Using the internet to network
- Mentors
- Affirmative action

- Female entrepreneurs
- Incentives and disincentives to self-employment
- The successful entrepreneur
- Are you a potential entrepreneur?
- The female entrepreneur
- Strengths / weaknesses of female entrepreneurs

- Types of self-employment
- Ten steps to a successful business
- Know your business
- Marketing, pricing, distribution, financing, business plan organising, staffing and managing staff
- Putting your dreams into action

INTRODUCTION

Initially, I began my research on this topic for a seminar I was going to call 'Escaping the Pink-Collar Ghetto.' After launching my seminar I realised from the response of my audiences, that there was a real need for this kind of book.

This book is intended for women who are frustrated in their attempts to climb the corporate ladder or who have hit a dead end in a pink-collar position. (A 'pink-collar' position is any office support position with low pay and few company benefits.) It will confirm the achievements of women who have successfully transcended their pink-collar positions and help women who feel trapped in such positions to use their abilities more effectively to get the kinds of positions they want.

I discuss management's point of view and show women many of the reasons why they're not being promoted. Numerous women are playing a losing game in business because they're 'playing basketball on a cricket field.' They simply don't know the rules for effective participation or the correct methods for climbing the corporate ladder.

During my research, I found many business women who had experienced the same feelings of frustration in the work world as I had. Unexpectedly, a number of men also called me to suggest I offer them a seminar on 'Escaping the Blue-Collar Ghetto.' They insisted that many men don't know the 'rules' either. Others suggested I put on seminars to teach men ways of dealing with the 'new woman' that would help them avoid offending her. They wanted to know the new rules as they relate to working with and interacting with women managers. It appears that men too are confused by recent changes and want to do the right thing.

Participants who attended my seminar were very enthusiastic. A frequent comment was, '*I just wish this seminar had been available to me fifteen years ago – I wouldn't have wasted so many years in a low-level position – I could have used my capabilities better.*'

Chapter One

On the home front

When problems arise at home, it's hard to concentrate at work - so before taking a peek at what you're doing in the work area of your life, let's examine what's happening with you on the home front.

Traditionally, women were the self-sacrificing nurturers in the family. However, in the last few decades this has changed, partly because of simple economics and partly because of the liberating effects of the women's movement. In the 80s many families simply couldn't survive financially with only one breadwinner and the situation hasn't changed since. Fewer women are willing (or able) to confine their priorities to marriage and child rearing, therefore more women are pursuing full-time careers. Presently, three out of every four women over the age of twenty and under sixty-five are in the workforce.

Where do you fit?

Each group of women has problems unique to it - whether they're single women, single mothers, married women, divorced or widowed or women who are empty nesters. If you're juggling family responsibilities with trying to get ahead in a career, the first question you must to ask yourself is: *'Will it be worth all the hard work and dedication I'll have to give if I want to climb the corporate ladder?'* You'll need to make a conscious decision about this - then prepare yourself to act on your decision. Being successful in a career is exhausting; it requires time, dedication, a good work ethic and *'the smarts.'* But it can be done!

Stay-at-home Moms

If you have tiny children at home, you might choose to say, *'They deserve my attention right now. They're my first priority, so I'm going to stay at home with them.'* That's fine. But don't just 'mark time' while you're at home.

Women are three times as likely as men to sacrifice their careers for the sake of marriage and child rearing, but young married women can no longer count on *being taken care of* by their husbands. Three

13

out of four women either never marry or lose their husbands through death, divorce or separation.

Many women follow their husband's wishes or choose not to work away from home for many years. Some may do occasional part-time work. However, if they had to return to full-time employment, they'd find themselves poorly prepared. If the woman's husband became ill or if he decided to go back to full-time college, university or for other upgrading reasons, she may need to be the breadwinner. Or she may find herself suddenly widowed or divorced and have no other choice but to return to the workplace. If she's not prepared - this can be devastating.

So, if you're a stay-at home Mom, make sure you keep yourself ready to go back to full-time employment if it became necessary. But why go back to a pink-ghetto position? Instead, prepare yourself to return to the workplace to an occupation you like and earn the salary you're worth. While you're still at home, start by obtaining career counselling to determine your skills and abilities. If you've found a good career counsellor, s/he will help you identify your transferrable skills and show many occupations you could go into that would use your unique skills and abilities. While you're at home, you could obtain the education or training you'd need to make the transition. Many courses can be taken in the evening, making it easier for your husband to take over the home and childcare responsibilities while you upgrade your skills.

The first step is to know where you want to go and what kind of occupation you want to enter when you decide to re-enter the workforce. Be sure to ask yourself, *'If I were a man, what kind of profession would I choose for myself?'* Remember that seldom, if ever, will a man choose a clerical or support position except when forced to do so. Keep this in mind when choosing your career. Be willing to start at the bottom of the ladder, but make sure there are well-identified rungs to climb to get where you ultimately want to be!

When I was young, I felt that there were few career options open to me - to become a nurse, a teacher, a secretary or, to become a mother. Even though my parents were open to my going to college or university, I chose to become a secretary, assuming that I'd probably follow my mother's footsteps and seldom, if ever, work outside the home after my children were born. I felt that obtaining a

14

career or university education would be a waste of time and money. What a mistake I made!

I stayed at home with my children during my marriage, but often found myself bored to tears. I'd wander around, wondering what else I could be doing with my time and talents. Instead of marking time, I could have spent time preparing for my re-entry to the work force. This would have also given me two major bonuses. By taking courses, I'd relieve the monotony of homemaking and child rearing and would have kept my mental faculties in a learning mode. Unfortunately, when I returned to work, I was forced to start all over and returned to a lower-level position than the one I'd left before having my children.

After two years of working in tedious pink-collar ghetto positions, I decided that if I was going to work for eight hours a day anyway, I wanted to be doing something I was good at - that I liked - and which would pay me enough to live the lifestyle I desired. I started by setting concrete career goals for myself.

Family as First Priority - But Must Work

Even among those women who choose family as their primary responsibility - many *have* to work for economic reasons. Often these women feel very guilty because of having to leave their children. They feel their place is with their children. While at work, they torture themselves with visions of their children getting into trouble. Or they believe that their children feel neglected or abandoned - simply because she's working.

There's good news for working mothers. Psychological studies show children of working mothers develop as well as (and sometimes better than) children with full-time mothers. It's how much a woman loves her children, how concerned and involved she's with them and how happy she is with *her* life (not whether she works or stays at home) that's important. Research also found that these children learn how to take responsibility, to do their share of home chores and are part of the family unit or 'team.' They also gain valuable social skills by spending more time with other children.

These women need to decide how much pressure they can tolerate in a position to be able to fulfil their obligations at home and at work. Many accept positions with low responsibility - ones that don't require much energy or input, but still bring home a paycheque. Once women decide to follow this route, they'll have to forego thoughts of progressing in their careers. Seldom (if ever) will they be considered for senior positions in a company and their chance of climbing the corporate ladder is almost nil. Therefore psychologically, they need to curtail their anxiety about staying where they are and be patient until their family responsibilities diminish before starting their own corporate climb up the ladder.

Career as main priority

If you've chosen to give priority to your career and have children, your first task is to obtain adequate care for them, so you can go to work with a clear conscience. You'll need to prepare yourself mentally for the guilt feelings you'll have or that others will try to thrust upon you because you've 'abandoned' your children. If guilt is holding you back, this book may help you find the answer to turning it off or at least easing some of your concerns.

Child Care

Working mothers need to know that their children are well cared for when they go to work each day. If this feeling of confidence is missing, they'll find it hard to concentrate on their work which will affect their promotional opportunities. So, if you're constantly worrying about what's happening to your children, make it a top priority to improve the situation. Examine the kind of care you're now providing for your children and identify alternatives to it. Only then will you be able to dedicate the kind of attention your job will require. Finding alternative childcare might be the answer that could involve:

- **Before and After School Care**

  This can be provided by a reliable neighbour, your school or possibly a community centre where the children can go before and after school.

- **Full-day Care for Pre-school Aged Children**

  This can be provided by a professional child-care service. The main advantage of day-care centres is your children learn how to socialise with other children.

16

A disadvantage of placing your children in professional child-care centres (be it part- or full-time) is that should one of your children become ill – the centre will probably refuse to accept that child for care. You'd have to make other arrangements for that child's care - possibly with a neighbour, relative or non-working friend until his or her health improved. Prepare for this eventuality, otherwise you may be placed in the position of missing work yourself (jeopardising your chances for advancement in your firm).

Many families find that the cost of day care takes too large a portion of their family's salary, especially if they're paying for more than one child at a day care centre.

- **Neighbours**

    Often neighbours who have young children of their own will care for your children while you work. This has the advantage of keeping your children close to home and helps with the socialisation of your child(ren).

- **Nanny**

    An alternative is to hire a 'nanny.' This nanny could either live in or come every morning before you head off to work and leave when you get home.

Some of the advantages of having a live-in nanny are:
- ✓ Younger children can sleep in,
- ✓ Person can assist older children to get ready for school.
- ✓ There's someone available should if-aged children become ill or need to go to the doctor or dentist and
- ✓ There's someone to care for older children before and after school.
- ✓ Live-in nannies may also prepare the family dinner and clean up afterwards. Because they live in your home, their actual salary isn't as high as you might imagine. It's certainly worth the effort to find out what you would have to pay for this type of assistance.

One disadvantage of this is that many nannies come from other cultures and speak with heavy accents that can affect the speech of very young children. They also have different ways of dealing with

17

ill children and have to learn how to use all the gadgets in the home. Another disadvantage of this kind of arrangement is the lack of privacy for the couple. One solution is to have the nanny live in five days of the week and spend weekends elsewhere. This gives the nanny some time off and ensures a measure of privacy for the couple.

Whichever method you choose - make sure you can leave home with a clear conscience. Always provide a number where you can be reached in case of emergency. This is where a mobile phone comes in handy because it keeps you in constant contact with your child care givers and doesn't tie up company phone lines.

How can you obtain your family's help at home?

If you don't have a nanny to do some of the household chores, you will be faced with the problem of being in two places at once - at work and at home. Your home situation has changed, so you'll need to decide which family responsibilities should be delegated to others. You'll require your spouse and children's reliable help and co-operation at home to accomplish this. If this help is not forthcoming, you'll probably have to hire someone to help you with the home and child-care responsibilities.

Research tells us that when men with traditional views marry, most have no intention of changing the routine of their lives. They figure that basically, they'll do the same things, think the same things and be the same person - but as a married - rather than a single man. In the past, women have often reshaped their personalities to conform to the wishes, needs and demands of their husbands, but this has changed in most households.

Does your husband 'help' around the house by taking out the garbage once a week? If so, here's an approach that might help you obtain the necessary assistance you'll need.

A recent survey shows unequivocally that women do the lion's share of the housework, at every stage of their lives - whether they're employed or not. Women have an hour less free time per day than men - at *every* stage of their lives. And once they have children, women normally do twice as much unpaid work (4.8 hours daily) than before they had children! No wonder working women are so tired!

18

On the other hand - when men become fathers, they do increase the amount of time they spend on unpaid work, but still work 1.7 hours less *per day* than their wives. One survey provided a surprising statistic. Fathers who have full-time working wives do *less* around the house than if their wives stayed at home. However, before the survey was conducted both the men and the women stated they were unaware of this. It was only after they both reported how they spent every hour of the previous day, that they learned the truth.

So, have a talk with him. Before you worked, you likely had distinct boundaries of responsibility. His responsibility was to be the breadwinner. Yours were to take care of the home and provide child-care. Things have changed. You're now sharing his traditional breadwinning role, so you need him to share the home-making and child-rearing role. It's as simple as that!

The belief that the family unit is breaking down is becoming increasingly wide-spread and the return of women to the workforce is often cited as the cause of this breakdown. The reality is, that families where the mothers work are more likely to work as a team and their children become responsible for doing their share of the chores.

Children who grow up to believe that Mom should make their beds, clear their dishes off the table or believe that as children they're on this earth to have nothing but fun - are being deprived of one of life's most important learning experiences. All overindulgence breeds, is spoiled, selfish children, who expect not only their teachers - but later employers - to give in to their every whim.

Parents should never do for children, what they can do for themselves.

If parents do, they'll only breed dependent, often demanding, children who expect a 'free ride' through life; who depend on external things to make them happy and wait for others to provide them with what they want. These individuals never acquire the exhilarating feeling of independence that comes from knowing they can do whatever is necessary to succeed.

Don't underestimate your children's abilities. Children become irresponsible only when parents fail to give them responsibility and the tools to fulfil their obligations.

19

Family Conferences

What if your family still won't help with chores? How do you get them to pitch in and do their share of the tasks? Have a family conference and use the following strategies:

1. Write down **all** the chores that need to be done around the house and yard. Include everything. Make a copy for each member of your family who is old enough to read.
2. Call a family conference (allow plenty of time).
3. At the family conference, ask for all members to *volunteer* to do some of the chores. Fill in the chores you feel comfortable handling yourself and have your spouse add his as well.
4. The remaining chores will then have to be assigned. (And don't let it be 'dear old Mom' who takes them on - because Mom doesn't have time either!) Even two-year-olds should have chores such as:
   - Picking up their own toys;
   - Putting their dirty clothes in clothes hamper;
   - Helping with dusting, making shelves and drawers neat or tidying shoes in a closet.

   Make sure your family knows you're counting on them to do their chores correctly *the first time*. Explain that you don't want to nag them to get their chores done. Confirm their understanding of what you want them to do. You may have to write a job description of exactly what you expect from them including how and when you expect their chores to be completed. Then ask: *'Can I count on you to do these chores?'* Get a verbal commitment from each of them. Then, like a supervisor - follow-up to make sure they do their chores properly.

5. Avoid power struggles. If children won't give you their word that they'll do a task, ask them why. Acknowledge their reason and reply, *'I know that taking out the garbage is not exactly a chore you like, but someone has to do it. Who do you think should be doing it?'* Be willing to negotiate, but be firm and identify what the consequences will be, if they do not complete their assignments. Be sure to follow through with your consequences if they renege.

6. Give rewards. Signs of love and appreciation are necessary. Adults are normally rewarded for work well done; children should be too. You might put a monetary value to the chores your children are expected to complete (in the form of an allowance) and deduct money for each breach of duty. Special family treats could be arranged for exceptional work.

7. Keep track of work completed. Make sure each child knows when duties are expected to be done. If they're constantly saying, *'I don't have time.'* help them plan their time.

8. Make sure children have the training they need to fulfil their obligations.

9. For particularly unpleasant tasks, have a rotation system where all family members capable of doing the chore, take their turn.

10. If fathers opt out of doing their share of home and child care duties and you're still doing your share, the salary of the person hired should be paid out of the husband's salary. If he objects, remind him of the principle of sharing breadwinner / homemaker responsibilities. Parenting is a dual responsibility and fathers should do their equal share in bringing up their children, plus their share of all the backbreaking work that goes along with the upkeep of a home.

11. If your family won't give a firm commitment to do the chores - you have two other choices. Hire someone else to help with the chores (which will reduce your family's overall income and cut children's allowances). Or you can quit your job (which will also reduce the family income). Whatever you decide, make sure your family knows the consequences of both these choices. Have them be part of the decision-making process by telling them the advantages they'll have if you work and the changes that will occur if you quit your job. You'll have to prepare for this before you call a family conference to discuss the issue and be ready for what they recommend for you to do.

12. If you take the time to write down the thousands of things you do for them, you'll be amazed. Simply stop doing some of them. Be reasonable. If you are - the chore will usually get done. If they refuse to help out - start removing privileges (no TV tonight). Or stop making their school lunches or driving them to their sporting events.

Husband objects to wife working

Do you have a traditionalist husband who still believes there should be only one breadwinner in the family - and that's him? Has he 'lost face' because it's now financially necessary for you to work?

Women should have the opportunity of pursuing a career, if that's their desire. Husbands who object to this are being very selfish. If you feel you're slowly losing your sanity and the four walls are closing in on you, try this approach. Ask your husband if he would like to exchange roles for a while. It's unlikely that he'd agree to do so, even though he jokingly will suggest that he'd love to have the opportunity of doing so.

Overcoming objections

1. Your husband says that after your expenses are paid, there won't be enough left out of your salary to make the 'disruption' worthwhile. The husband's objection goes as follows, *'Are you crazy? We can't afford to do that! If we both work, it'll put me into another income tax bracket.'* Explain that you *need* to work - that you're going into a low-level position now but with training and education you hope to reach a higher salary level soon. (Employees normally start at the bottom and you can't expect to get to the top right away). Most income-tax specialists agree that the extra income tax involved is more than compensated by the income earned by the wife.

2. Your parents, your in-laws and non-working female friends offer a variety of guilt-generating reasons why you shouldn't return to work or go back to school for upgrading. *'Your kids need you, depend on you ...'* Or, *'Why did you have kids in the first place if all you wanted was to educate yourself and go back to work?'* You should:
   a) Recognise they don't have the right to tell you what you should or shouldn't do with your life. After weighing all the factors, *you and only you* should make that decision
   b) Refuse to accept the guilt trips they're thrusting upon you. Your happiness spreads to your family. This is not a selfish wish. It's a necessity for your personal happiness.

3. Your husband would prefer that you did volunteer work where you'll be away only part-time. You should:

   a) Explain your need to do something that suits *your* needs - not his.

   b) Explain the benefits he and the children will have because you'll be happier.

4. Your husband says he's afraid that working all day will be too tiring for you. Remind him that he has probably seen you get crankier and crankier, more and more tired around the home. He hasn't put two and two together to understand your crankiness and your tiredness go hand in hand with your boredom. Explain this to him.

5. Your husband says it's okay for you to return to work, but you shouldn't expect him to help out much. He's too tired already when he comes home. Then hire someone to do his share of the housework and child rearing, to be paid out of *his* salary.

6. Your husband says he already 'helps' around the house. After all, doesn't he help clear the table after dinner and take out the garbage? You can explain that he isn't helping you - he's helping himself. It's *his* responsibility to do whatever is necessary around the house to get all the jobs done. This is not helping you; it's doing his share of the work. Don't ask him to *'Help you with ...'* He should be made to feel he's *'Helping himself with ...'*

7. You accept a position at the same salary as his. You're climbing fast, but he's hit a snag in promotional opportunities. He's starting to show anxiety that you'll overtake him and upset the balance of family power. This anxiety is revealed in a variety of ways. He may start belittling you or try to sabotage your career by making you choose between your professional goals and his demands. Or he may stop 'helping' around the home, will withhold sex, become emotionally abusive or look to other women to boost his male ego.

8. Ignoring this situation certainly won't help. As one of the more intractable problems of the two-career couple; this is probably worth a book of its own. Most men are raised to believe that they'll have to support a family. Because promotions mean more money, they're willing to make sacrifices to reach the top. Unfortunately, a woman in the same position is frowned upon because she has not put her family first. Start by discussing the problem openly with him. You may need to seek professional counselling to find a solution.

Giving loving time to your family

Most working women, who are parents of young children, face the following questions:

1. When time is at a premium - how do I provide quality time with my children?
2. How can I make sure my children get the love and attention they need when I'm away from home over eight hours a day?

A conscious, planned effort must be made to provide this care without the guilt that often goes along with it. *Both* parents need to do the following:

- Spend individual time with each child that the child thinks of as his or her 'special' time with the parent. This can be ten to fifteen minutes each day and a set time on the weekend.

- Keep track of your children's 'other lives' - at the baby-sitter, the day-care centre, kindergarten, school, sports and artistic activities, etc. Learn about special events at school and take time to attend. Encourage your children to keep you informed.

- Practice effective listening and try not to be judgmental. Don't let time with your children become an inquisition. Hear what your children are *not* saying, by watching their body language and non-verbal communication.

- Enlist your children's help or ask for their presence when you're doing chores, so you can chat with them and discuss their day.

- Use effective time planning to eliminate unnecessary steps and tasks in order to give yourself more time with your family. Establish priorities and remember to put spending quality time with your children high on this list.

- Plan special outings that cater to individual needs. At a family conference, have each member state the special things s/he likes to do as a family. Try to utilise this list when planning special outings.

- Be aware of your own stress level so you don't over-react to minor incidents with your children. If you've had a bad day at work, explain this to your children and ask if you can talk to them later. Don't put them off too long. Follow up on things they need to discuss with you.

- Don't feel guilty when you need 'private time' and remember to honour your children's need for privacy too.

Consider the following questions:

1. Do you feel you provide quality time with your children?
2. Do you feel effective as a parent?
3. What immediate steps could you take to change #1 and #2?

If you answer no to any of the above, I recommend that you read Dr. Thomas Gordon's book: *Parent Effectiveness Training (P.E.T.).*

Husband's Quality Time

And don't forget about your husband - he needs your quality time too. Plan some *wicked weekends* and *couple holidays* (without your children) so the two of you can rekindle the feelings of your early romantic days. Arrange often to go on *dates.* Fuss and primp in preparation for these occasions (the way you did earlier in your marriage). Otherwise, your marriage might become nothing but work, work and more work. You need some time off without the responsibilities of your children and to allow yourself to let the 'little kid' in you out to play.

Equality

Do working men and women face the same problems relating to their work lives? Usually *No.* Consider the following example:

Two employees working for a company are given the same assignment. One is a woman, the other a man. Each is married, with a fourteen-year-old son and a nine-year-old daughter. It's 2:00 pm. An important meeting has been arranged for 9:00 am in another city tomorrow. It's necessary for each employee to leave that evening on the 9 o'clock plane. There are no problems for the woman at work - her problems occur at home.

Male: Phones spouse tells her about his trip
Female: Phones spouse tells him about her trip;

Male: 6 pm wife serves <u>his</u> dinner;
Female: 6 pm eats dinner <u>she</u> has prepared.

Male: Wife checks list of items he's to take;
Female: Checks list of items she must take with her;

Male: Wife helps pack his bag;
Female: Packs own suitcase;

Male: Wife asks if he wants a ride to airport;
Female: She calls a cab so he can stay with the kids;

They return from their trips the next evening at 8 pm. Both are exhausted and bone weary. Neither has eaten much since noon, (mouths are watering for a ham sandwich). They enter their front door:

Male: Wife greets him at the door with, *'Hi Hon!'* Gives him a kiss and asks about his trip; Children yell, *'Hi Dad!'*
Female: Husband watching TV yells, *'Hi Hon!'* Children meet their mother and describe what went wrong with their day.

Male: She hangs up <u>his</u> coat;
Female: She hangs up <u>her</u> coat;

Male: He flops into chair in living room explaining how tired he is;
Female: She flops into chair in living room explaining how tired she is;

Male: Wife asks if he's eaten yet;
Female: Asks, *'Have you guys eaten yet?'*

Male: Wife makes him a ham sandwich and tea;
Female: Makes herself tea and a ham sandwich. Her son sees it and asks her to make him one too; followed soon after by her daughter (they explain that they've only had soup and toast for dinner). Her husband leaves the TV to ask for one too. No ham left - she has tea and toast;

Male: Wife unpacks <u>his</u> suitcase, finds a spilled bottle of after shave. Wife washes contents of his suitcase.
Female: Unpacks <u>her</u> suitcase, finds a spilled bottle of hand cream. She washes the contents of her suitcase.

Male: Wife goes to bed, feels amorous towards him, but knows how tired he is. She covers him up and lets him sleep.

Female: Husband goes to bed, feels amorous towards wife and starts making advances. She mumbles, *'I'm too tired tonight'*. She's shocked by his next comment, *'I told you this job would be too much for you!'*

Many men's lives are made a lot easier by the fact that they come home to a caring, nurturing, empathetic partner. This partner is called a *wife*. It's unfortunate that women don't have this luxury! If they did, half their frustrations and feelings that there's something missing in their lives would be gone. To learn more about this topic, read **What Do Women Want? - Exploding the Myth of Dependency**, by Luise Eichenbaum & Susie Orbach.

Are you one of the lucky women who have a 'wife' (a helpful, nurturing husband) at home? Many men are learning that nurturing doesn't have to be an exclusively feminine trait, but it can be a very masculine trait as well. Many men are learning how to nurture and be more empathetic towards others. For instance, when their wives come dragging in from work, these men say, *'Had a tough day? How about a cup of tea or a glass of wine?'* Or, *'Do you want half an hour to yourself while I fix dinner?'* Isn't this what a wife does? Wouldn't it be wonderful if all working women had that luxury?

A man with these qualities usually had a mother who cared about him enough to teach him that he can show empathy and tenderness to those he loves and cares about - without losing his masculinity. The man who doesn't have these qualities has probably been trained since childhood *not* to have them. Many younger men have acquired this quality because they've observed their mothers working and know what a toll it took on their energies

Women need to have this kind of flexibility too. They should be the *'husband'* at times and do some of the traditionally male jobs. They can carry the two-by-fours, use the paintbrush or roller and do the kinds of chores husbands are traditionally expected to do. Women can do most of these tasks - if they make the effort. Women can't expect men to change, if they're not willing to reciprocate.

Besides, any shared chore is more fun. It isn't just the man's job to paint. If you have a bedroom to paint, share the sanding and painting. If the yard needs raking - join in. If a family works as a team - the job is completed in half the time.

Carol Gilligan, a psychologist and author of *In a Different Voice*, observes that girls tend to be trained by their mothers to sense others' needs. They see themselves as part of a web of relationships. Meanwhile, many boys learn from their fathers to seek independent achievement and that tying themselves too closely to others will threaten their self-esteem.

To most wives, intimacy means sharing feelings. To most husbands it means sharing activities - going to a movie together, for example. When he's watching television, he wants her close by and wonders why she chooses to phone a friend. She can't understand why he's upset if she does this, when he's not paying any attention to her. Many wives find their female friends make better confidantes than their husbands. Quite often women live together because they provide 'wifing' or nurturing for each other.

Obtain a copy of Eichenbaum and Orbach's: *What Do Women Want* and give it to the men in your life. It's for husbands, lovers, fathers and sons. Before reading this book, few men really understand the meaning of the word 'nurturing' because their mothers neglected to give them this essential training. Until recently, I didn't understand the empty feeling I'd often experienced during my adult life. I always had the feeling that something important was missing in my life. Even when I was married or with a close male friend, there always seemed to be something lacking in the relationship. I hadn't connected this to not having a man in my life who was willing to nurture and help me in the way I'd be willing to help him. Most women find this kind of nurturing through their female friends, so cultivate a few who can fill this void in your life instead of counting on the man or men in their life to provide it.

Another essential book for both men and women to read (and especially women in the workplace) is John Gray's *Men are from Mars, Women are from Venus* which explains communication differences between men and women.

Introducing Business to Home Management

Life runs smoothly at the office - why does it fall apart at home? Where's the gas bill? When is Sally's next dentist appointment? What groceries do I have to pick up on my way home from work? When you have a dual lifestyle, balancing a career and home duties -

it's usually the home front that does you in. Learn to use business techniques in the home as well.

Planning is essential for getting your homemaking chores under control. Use lists for everything - grocery bill - things that need doing around the house and yard (and who is expected to do them!). Learn to set priorities. Is it really more important to have a spotless house or to spend an hour teaching Sally how to knit? Know the things that are important to you and what you can let slide when more important priorities come along. Your lists should be divided into:

- Have to: (Priority As)
- Need to: (Priority Bs)
- Hope to: (Priority Cs)
- Forget it: (Priority Ds)

And find time for yourself - to do the things of importance to you. This is usually low on most working women's list of priorities, but in reality should be near the top. Wise parents learn that they must be what they would term as 'selfish' and do special things for themselves - in order to be more effective in dealing with all aspects of their lives. Putting yourself number 'one' is *not* a sin - it is a necessity (providing you don't take it to the extreme).

Delegate jobs to your family and follow up. That is the essential ingredient of delegation - follow-up. This is done to ensure that the job is being done properly, to give praise for a job well done and help in improving the quality of the performance. Have a plan set up as to what you will do if the job is not done. Be consistent with discipline and fair to all members of your family.

Use the Swiss Cheese Approach (take little bites out of tasks) in family chores. Wallpapering the kitchen takes planning and can be done with 'Instant Tasks' (soaking the wallpaper with warm water could be one).

When cooking - make multiple batches. It takes just a little longer to make meals for four days than just for one. Utilise your freezer as much as possible. Stop wasting your time picking up groceries every second day - make fewer trips.

Some leave most of the family chores until the weekend, but find that their family doesn't have time to do things together. One woman

29

corrected this, by doing her shopping on Thursday evening and did a load of wash every day while she was preparing, serving and cleaning up for dinner. This eliminated the six batches she usually did on Saturday, which used to tie her to her home unless she did it all at a laundromat.

Hire a student to do the jobs that pile up - cut the grass, paint the fence, shovel the driveway or help with the spring cleaning.

During the children's summer holidays, consider hiring a 'mother's helper' so that babysitting and home care can be accomplished at one time. Screen applicants for this position carefully - choose the person who has a genuine liking for children and does a good job around the house. Ask questions about how they would deal with emergencies. Do your homework and have emergency phone numbers ready for your substitute parent.

Leave 'chore' lists for your children of what you expect them to do during the day while you're at work. Make them feel part of a team - that they're contributing something valuable to the family unit. Plan special treats to reward good performance.

Which Career Choice is Best for You?

Decide how important your career is to you and what is best for you and your unique circumstances. You may want to 'mark time' while your children are young or simply don't want the hassles that promotions warrant. You must feel comfortable about your choice, no matter which decision you make. The important thing is that *you* choose what's best for *you* - this decision shouldn't be made *for* you by others. Whatever you decide to do, the maze of corporate gamesmanship will make more sense to you after you read the next chapter.

Chapter Two

Why managers say they don't promote women

As part of the research for this book, I interviewed over seven hundred managers to find out why they weren't promoting more women into management or decision-making positions. Many of their reasons were very valid and women wishing to get ahead would be wise to listen to their explanations. These are things women have the ability to change - things women are doing that are holding *themselves* back.

Women are often tempted to point to male chauvinism as the only reason why they aren't being promoted, but as we'll see, only about twenty percent of the problems can be attributed to chauvinism (be it male or female); the other eighty percent is up to the women themselves. Here are the findings from my interviews. After each barrier you will find steps to take to eliminate those barriers.

Barriers to Promotion

1. Women haven't set concrete career goals for themselves.

How can a manager help a woman get where she wants to go - when she hasn't a clue where she wants to go in the first place? To succeed in life, whether it's to achieve something in one's personal or career lives - goals must be set and steps taken to ensure that those goals are met. This is just as important for women, as it is for men, but unfortunately, many women do not place enough importance on setting goals. Part of their goals should be to obtain career counselling so they know where they want to go in business. This topic will be discussed in greater detail in Chapter 4.

<u>Step #1:</u> Set career goals - obtain career counselling

2. Women have problems working overtime and travelling on business when necessary.

Women also have problems relocating when a promotional opportunity is available. These three related problems are close to the top of managers' lists of things holding women back from

31

promotions. Why should their companies expect male managers to work overtime and travel at the drop of a hat and not their female managers? Why should their companies only consider them for promotions that are within their own city? What makes them so special that these concessions should be made for them?

Ask yourself the following:

a) Have you refused to work overtime because of family commitments? Have you given the excuse, *'But who will pick Jenny up at the day care centre?'* If that was your reply, then unintentionally, you've silently told your employer *'Don't promote me - ever!'* Your employer will probably overlook you as a serious candidate for a promotion. What arrangements should you be making now, so that if you're asked to work overtime in the future - you'll be able to say, *'Give me a few minutes and I'll make the arrangements'?*

Step #2: Arrange childcare for when you have to work overtime

b) Have you refused to travel overnight or longer to another city due to family commitments? Has your reply to that request been, *'But who would look after my children?'* Again, without meaning to do so, you've again told your employer *'Don't promote me - ever.'* What plans could you make, so you could reply, *'Yes I can. Let me make the arrangements.'* This is especially difficult for single parents who do not have a partner available to take over the child-care duties.

Step #3: Arrange childcare for when you must travel

c) What would happen if your company offered you a promotion in another city? Would you have to refuse the offer (therefore again taking yourself out of the promotional loop)? What plans should you be making now to take care of this possibility?

Step #4: Talk to your husband and family about this issue. Know how they feel about re-location

What would your spouse say if:

1. You were asked to work overtime. Would he take over with the childcare responsibilities?
2. You had to travel to another city for a few days. Would he pitch in and take over your home and childcare responsibilities? Would he do this willingly?
3. How would he react if your company offered you a promotion in another city?

If you are a single parent:

1. Do you have someone who can step in if you had to work overtime?
2. Do you have someone who can step in if you had to travel overnight or for a few days?
3. Have you given thought as to what you would do if your company offered you a position in another city?

Prepare for the eventuality that you may face all three decisions in your climb up the corporate ladder and be sure you've formulated a plan of action where your spouse or someone else would take over your home and child-care responsibilities. Discuss these three issues with your husband so you know what to expect from him and what kind of assistance he'll provide (without grumbling). If he won't co-operate for the first two (overtime and business travel) what kind of alternative arrangements could you make? If the promotion to another city meets with resistance, you have two other choices - go without him or say 'No' to your employer. Then be prepared for the backlash of either eventuality.

Make sure your employer knows that overtime, travel and relocation are *not* problems for you. *Don't assume s/he knows this.*

3. Women are away from work too often because of their own or their children's illnesses.

Employment records show that on the average, women take sick leave about the same as men. However, they're absent more often than men because of their children's illnesses. Ask yourself the following questions:

a) In the last year, how much time have I taken off work because of my children's illnesses or because I had to take them to doctor's or dentist's appointments? Many mothers feel guilty if they don't take their children to doctor's appointments or stay home to look after their children when they're sick. That's why it's so important to have competent backup child-care available. You would have to arrange for in-home help, because day-care facilities won't accept a child with, say, the measles. The elderly widow down the street may not be suitable for full-time babysitting, but she may be ideal for this kind of emergency.

Have your backup person available to take your child to the doctor or dentist as well. Or learn whether your doctor, dentist or health unit has weekend or evening hours. Always have somebody available to help out - your husband, your mother or your aunt. But *do* have backup!

If there's an emergency and the child is really ill, your employer will accept your absence much more readily if your child-related absences have been infrequent. But, giving the excuse, *'Johnny's got a cold, so I'll stay home'* is not likely to endear you to management (especially when you're in line for a promotional opportunity). They'd be justified in saying, *'Forget about promoting her. She's away too often. She has children at home and she's not there when we need her.'*

Step #5: Ensure you have alternative childcare when children are sick or must see a doctor or dentist

b) How much time do you take off work because of your own illnesses? I don't mean when you have to miss work because of surgery or a bout of pneumonia. That isn't the kind of absenteeism that bothers employers (unless it's chronic and long-term). I'm talking about the casual illnesses where you're away one or two days a month. When you get into management positions, you're expected to be there! They rely on you. If you're absent too often, you're simply going to be overlooked for a promotion. It costs the company too much money to pay you while you're away. Remember - you'll be earning more money, so it costs your company more money each time you're away.

If you're moving towards a management position, have *female problems* and are away one or two days a month - don't *ever* give

34

that as your excuse for being away! If you have chronic female problems, see a doctor and obtain treatment. If you suffer from pre-menstrual tension, you'll be familiar with its symptoms; jumpiness, emotional upheaval, severe mood swings, cramping or depression. See your doctor and get the treatment you need. There's no need to suffer from these kinds of symptoms in this day of enlightened medicine. Don't give men in the office the chance to say things like, *'It's her time of the month again!'* If your superiors see you taking a day or so every month for your *female complaints* or witness you when you're on an emotional roller coaster, they'll likely decide they can't promote you.

If, on the other hand, you're being held back from a promotion and your attendance is excellent, make sure your employer knows about it by saying *'I was overlooked for a promotion and I'd like to find out why. It certainly couldn't be because of my attendance.'* But if you *are* away too often - you haven't a leg to stand on. They have the right *not* to promote you if your attendance is poor.

Step #6: See a doctor if you have 'female problems'

4. Women don't know their limitations and attempt to be Super-woman, Super-manager and Super-mom.

Managers know that unless their female employees with children have adequate help at home, they're likely working two full-time jobs - not one. Because they've seen it happen to their own wives or family members, they know that these women can't survive under these conditions long before they are likely to burn out.

If these women were asked which part of their lives caused them the most time management problems:

- Their work or business life;
- Their home or family life;
- Their social or community life.

They'd laugh. *'What social life? What community life? I only have time for the first two and even that is crammed full to the brim!'* To some, having private time by themselves is a luxury they seldom enjoy. Others find that they haven't been out socially with their friends for several weeks. Unless people balance their lives by paying close attention to all three areas of their lives, they'll end up

35

cheating themselves and their families. What's the sense of working *that* hard, if they can't enjoy life? So, if you find yourself still doing chores until it's time to go to bed (and get up the next day and do it all over again) ask yourself why you're behaving that way! Don't drag yourself to work in the morning or drag out at night. Trying to be superhuman is the biggest failing of women who are pursuing a career. They try *so* hard to be perfect at everything, that there's nothing left for just *living* and enjoying what their toil has brought them.

Are you trying to fill all three slots at once - wife, mother and career woman? Isn't it time you sat down with your family and divided the chores or hired someone to do some of them? Also make sure you take time to let your own 'little kid' out and allow yourself some play time - to socialise or simply goof-off if you feel like it. You've earned it! Everyone benefits if you're a relaxed, happy wife, mother and employee.

Keep your employer informed. Let your boss know you have competent help at home and that you're capable of handling not only your existing position, but other more complicated positions as well.

Step #7: Obtain help at home

5. Women bring their family and personal problems to work and waste time discussing them and worrying about them.

Learn to compartmentalise your life. Turn a mental switch 'off' when you leave home. If your children are properly cared for, you should be able to turn their problems 'off' when you leave them. If you had an argument with your spouse, turn that 'off' too. Concentrate instead, on matters related to your job. Do the same thing when you come home - turn the work switch 'off' and your home switch 'on.'

Make a conscious effort to do this. It's deadly to be pre-occupied, either at home or at work. Your work will suffer because of your lower concentration level. If you take a work problem home and little Margie is talking to you about something of importance to her, she knows when you're not really listening to her. Strive to give quality time both at work and at home by keeping both worlds separate.

You'll also notice that male supervisors and managers *do not* normally talk about their personal lives at work. Neither should you.

Step #8: Compartmentalise your life – 'on' and 'off'

How much of your time do you spend discussing personal matters at work? For example, *'My daughter Patti broke up with her boyfriend and she's very depressed ...'* Or, *'Bob and I had an argument this morning ...'*

How do you rate? Is this one of your failings? Managers are watching - and what do they see? They see dollar signs and these dollar signs are flying out the window. You're wasting not only your own time but that of the person you're talking to. Suppose you and your co-worker are earning twenty dollars hour. If the two of you spend just fifteen minutes per day in idle chatter, you've cost the company ten dollars worth of productivity. Multiply that by two hundred working days and you'll see that you're wasting about two thousand dollars of your company's money a year! That's what managers see. If you hope to be promoted - don't talk about *anything* except work-related matters during business hours. If you must talk about something that happened on the weekend - do it at coffee or lunch breaks.

Step #9: Don't waste company time on 'small talk'

How many personal phone calls do you make a day? If your children 'check in' with you when they arrive home from school - that's fine - as long as it isn't a long conversation. And beware of getting involved in domestic battles between two siblings who want you to referee their fights.

Step #10: Don't make unnecessary personal phone calls

6. Women gossip.

It's been said that people who gossip usually end up in their own mouth traps. It is a bad habit with many women - especially those who don't wish to get promoted in business. For women who are trying to get ahead, gossiping at work is an absolute no-no.

'What about the men who gossip?' you may ask. Chances are they aren't in management positions either. So refuse to participate in this destructive habit.

Step #11: Don't gossip!

7. Women don't stand up for their ideas and are afraid of confrontation.

Women have traditionally been the peacemakers in history and have considerable trouble shirking this assumed responsibility. Men are familiar with confrontation and find it stimulating to have a lengthy debate.

Unfortunately, women feel uncomfortable and aggressive when they're forced to defend their ideas, so they back off. A common reason why women fail in confrontational situations is that they neglect to take enough time to prepare their rebuttal so that they can back up their positions with facts rather than emotions. Instead, they make the mistake of starting their comments with, *'I think ... I feel ... Or, I believe ...'* Their suggestions cannot succeed if they use assumptions and/or guesswork.

Women also need to be ready with plan 'b' and plan 'c' should plan 'a' not succeed. These extra plans are developed by brainstorming so they'll have as many solutions as possible to try. Then they'd take the best solution and try it out, but have others as backup if the first one doesn't work. Sometimes they may have to look at the whole problem in a different light and rethink it completely.

Step #12: Defend your ideas. Take an assertiveness training course

8. Women with low self-esteem and self-confidence are afraid to take risks and try new things.

We'll be discussing this issue in more detail in Chapter 10.

Step #13: Same as #12

9. Women are poor communicators and are misunderstood too often.

38

I don't agree with management on this one. Women are far better communicators than most of their male counterparts. They communicate on a plane far above the level of most men, mainly because they use more communication methods. Some men become confused when women use these extra communication tools.

Women gain these extra communication skills through mothering. Think of the young mother with her child who's too young to talk. She uses two distinct communication skills that she hones to perfection; empathy (she puts herself in the place of the child) and her ability to read the child's body language. Some men are making an honest effort to acquire these skills (perhaps because they're accepting more responsibility in the caring for their children). When they bring these skills into the workplace - everyone benefits. Many men are copying these methods simply because they work.

For example: Two supervisors (one a male, the other a female) have been observing a staff member who is having a very difficult day. Anything that could have gone wrong has gone wrong, causing her to get behind in her work. Both supervisors must delegate a rush job to this employee. The male supervisor approaches the worker and says, *'I need this rush job done by 4:00 pm. I need you to leave all your other work and concentrate on this job.'*

The female supervisor (using empathy and understanding her body language) will say, *'I can see you're having a terrible day, but I need this rush assignment done by 4:00 pm. Don't worry about your other assignments – just concentrate on this task. Let me know if you run into any difficulties.'*

Which boss would you prefer to work for?

Step #14: Keep improving your communication skills

10. If their ideas are shot down, women act as if they are failures.

Men take rejection of an idea as part of the 'game.' However, if a woman gives a suggestion to her boss and has it rejected, she feels hurt. So instead of coming back with another idea that *will* work, she stops giving suggestions. Remember, the boss is rejecting *her idea*, not *her*! That's not what was intended by the rejection of her idea.

Women, unfortunately, take this kind of rejection personally. If they have an idea turned down, some respond with, *'Nobody's listening to my ideas - so why should I bother giving more?'*

If she doesn't come up with a second and possibly a third suggestion, she'll be seen by men as being a 'sissy' (a most derogatory term when aimed at men) because she gave up. She may revise her original suggestion, but she needs to keep on trying to find a plan that *will* work.

Step #15: Have plan 'b' and 'c' ready

11. Women have indirect ways of getting what they want - using 'female tricks' such as crying, pouting, having temper tantrums, acting cute or seductive.

These are manipulative ploys that some women believe will work. But they don't and women put themselves in an unfavourable position when they use these tactics. Honest communication is essential for success - no game playing. Learn to ask for things directly, instead of playing manipulative games.

The first one is crying. Bosses frown on women's tears in the workplace. (Unfortunately, women cry four times more often than men). It used to be thought that if a female broke down and bawled, it was *just the way women are,* which provided an excellent excuse for keeping them out of executive offices. The rules of business say that you simply don't cry. (Men don't know how to deal with it). Most women executives are never caught crying. They've become tough enough emotionally to save their tears for somewhere other than the workplace even if it's in the women's washroom.

The next is tantrums. Men are more likely to show their emotions through aggression. They'll yell, kick the garbage can or punch the wall - but they won't cry! This reaction is just as bad (or worse) than crying, but seems to be tolerated by men in the workplace. Most adults can control their reactions - but some men and women never master this skill. Instead they resort to having tantrums. These immature, insecure people have learned that if they kick up enough fuss, they'll get their way. They've used these tactics since childhood and because they still work with some people, they continue to use them especially when they're tired or have run into what they see as insurmountable obstacles. No matter what the reason, these tactics are not only childish but very disruptive in an office setting. These people don't seem to realise how much their behaviour disgusts others and those in management can't help but notice their off-the-wall behaviour. They need to grow up.

Then there are women who act cute or use seduction in the workplace. Every office seems to have one of these pieces of fluff. These women wear either frilly little-girl outfits, dress seductively or use the 'poor helpless me' approach. Some turn out to be good workers, but if they are promoted, others assume it's because they seduced someone in the company to get ahead.

Businesses are looking for professionalism and there's nothing professional about this kind of behaviour or ways of dressing. Ask yourself whether you want people to see you predominantly as a businesswoman or as a female. Chapter 10 will discuss this further.

Step #16: Don't use 'female tricks'

12. Women sabotage other women when they're promoted.

Some women sabotage other women when they've been promoted into a position of power or into the ranks dominated by men. This will be discussed in greater detail in Chapter 8.

Step #17: Support other female supervisors/managers

13. Women are unable to make independent decisions when necessary.

Ask yourself, *'When I have a major decision to make, either at work or in my private life, how many people do I consult before I actually make the decision?'* I can almost guarantee (unless you've already learned how to make independent decisions) that you'll consult at least one other person, whether it's a girlfriend, a husband, a boss or a workmate. You probably feel you *have* to get someone else's approval before taking that decision-making step. Certainly get information from others upon which to base the decision, but don't be afraid to make decisions. Use your intuition. If it feels right, run with it.

Unfortunately, some women stay clear of making decisions and expect others to make them for them. If you haven't read: *The*

Cinderella Complex by Colette Dowling, do so. Dowling discusses why women are often dependent on others to make their decisions for them and how this early social conditioning can be overcome. Women need to know that it's okay to make their own decisions, that it's their right and that it's necessary for them to succeed at any level of business.

Traditionally, women are expected from childhood to rely first on their parents and then on their husbands for confirmation of every decision they make. They learned to feel inadequate and incapable of making correct decisions. Therefore, these women feel they must get the advice of at least one other person before they make any major decision. I encourage all women to live on their own before they marry. This ensures that they'll learn how to make independent decisions. Otherwise, they'll likely go from one dependent situation into another, without trying their wings and proving they can 'fly' alone.

Dowling goes on to explain that she was very capable of making decisions as long as there was no male around. As soon as a man entered her life, she forfeited that decision-making right to the fellow she was with. When I read her book, I realised that I too, had been making decisions for myself and my children since my divorce without consulting anyone; but as soon as a significant man came into my life, I turned my decision-making rights over to him. I doubt that he wanted it.

Dependent women *expect* others to look after them and wait for something external to change their lives. Setting goals for themselves is out of the question, unless someone else advises them and helps them do it. These women seldom have to make decisions until their spouse dies or they become divorced. Even when they're on their own, they find themselves looking for someone who can make their decisions for them. When they remarry, they relinquish decision-making again.

This conditioning of women to rely on others is often brought into the business world. It's common for women to procrastinate, using a variety of excuses to avoid the responsibility of making a decision. Managers are right when they say that few women are able to make decisions without involving others.

So how can you change? Practice making small decisions, before tackling the big ones. When you find yourself faced with making a decision, fight the urge to involve someone else in the decision-making process. Have faith in your ability to make the right decision. Start the decision-making by writing things down. First, write down all the possible decisions you could make. Then note all the pros and cons of each decision - then choose the best one.

Now, devise a step-by-step plan of action on how you'll make your decision happen. Companies value this talent and look for this ability in their managers.

Step #18: Learn how to make decisions without the help of others

We've discussed the reasons managers gave for not promoting women. Here are things managers admitted *they* might be doing - often unconsciously - to hold women back in business:

1. Some male managers overlook women for promotion out of protectiveness.

Because men are taught traditionally that it's their duty to protect women and be the decision makers, many feel very uncomfortable placing a woman in a decision-making position. Others won't consider women for promotions because they want to protect them from the heavy demands of management. This is not done to put women down, but because they feel women must be sheltered.

Women need to show this type of manager that they're fully prepared to take on the role of a supervisor or manager by making sure they are fully trained *before* they apply for a supervisory or management position. If necessary, women should be prepared to spend their own money to accomplish this, because their company will likely pay for the training after they're in the position. (This is what I did when I was climbing the corporate ladder. Each time I spent money on training, my company later paid for it.)

The next step is to prepare a list of the major decisions they've made in their past employment and be ready to explain how their talents and abilities can help the company. To aid in this, they should obtain career counselling to learn all about the transferrable skills they bring to their employer and their likelihood of succeeding in a supervisory or management role.

Step #19: Make sure your boss knows your career plans

2. Some male managers over-train women before they set them free to use their training.

Managers seem to think that women require twice as much on-the-job training as men before they're ready for their next promotion. But if managers looked closely, they'd see that many women train the people who ultimately get promoted.

For instance, a young man (fresh out of university) starts with the company, is trained by a senior personal assistant (possibly you) and climbs his way up the ladder to management. Your bosses, by the way, love having you where you are. You provide them with the best training resource of all and you're inexpensive to boot! Without you they'd have to pay a fortune for this type of on-the-job training! Know your worth. Your employer would be foolish to promote you under these conditions. So it's up to you to take steps to stop this from happening in the future and apply for the next promotion yourself.

Explain your situation to your boss by saying, *'This isn't right! I've trained Harry - I've trained Joe - and I've trained Bill. If I was capable of training them, why am I being overlooked for a promotion? I'm capable of climbing that ladder myself.'* Then listen to what your boss has to say. If further education or training is necessary - get it!

It's up to you, to let your boss know that you don't like being overlooked (you'll keep getting overlooked as long as you remain silent). Stand up for what you feel is right and fair - but by using facts, not emotions. Let your boss know that you want to be considered for the next promotion. Explain *why* you think you deserve the promotion. Ask what's missing in your background that would improve your promotional chances. See Chapter 6 for more information on this issue.

Step #20: Stand up for yourself. Make sure your company treats you fairly

3. Some Managers promote women into positions for which they have had little or no training.

This almost argues with what I've been saying, but, more women than men are thrown into supervisory positions without supervisory training. Many are initially appointed as clerical supervisor or office manager, so management assumes training isn't necessary. But *any* supervisory job requires supervisory training to be done properly. More about supervision in Chapter 7.

<u>Step #21</u>: Obtain supervisory training before accepting any supervisory position

4. Some managers fail to provide up-to-date job descriptions.

Many positions lack job descriptions, so the employee wanders around trying to decide what she's expected to do. You often hear new employees say, *'Oh was I supposed to do that?'* Even their bosses may not know all the duties of the job, because they may not have worked closely with the former employee. So the new staff member is forced to re-invent the wheel especially if her predecessor left before she started working in the position.

If you're placed in the position of not knowing specifically what you're supposed to do, ask your boss for a written job description. Find out what your priorities are and specifically what your boss wants from you. How can your boss possibly do a performance appraisal and evaluate how well you do your job, if neither of you knows what you're supposed to do? Therefore, every position (not just groups of positions) requires an accurate, up-to-date job descriptions that include Key Performance Indicators; the tasks required to achieve those KPIs and standards of performance or competencies (that include how, when, where, quality, quantity and time) for each task performed.

Many companies will give the excuse, *'Well we don't have job descriptions in this company.'* Then write your own and have your boss go through it with you so you'll both know what's expected of you. If you supervise others, help them write theirs so you can monitor how well they're doing. This can be done even in a company that *'Doesn't have job descriptions'*

Remember, it's the position you describe in a job description - not the person in it. Except in highly progressive companies, employees are hired to fill a position - not the other way around where the position is adapted to suit the applicant.

Step #22: Make sure you have an accurate up-to-date job description

5. Women are discouraged from imitating men in business and told to use their 'unique' talents and abilities instead.

Many top management people state that women *can* act differently from men in business. This is generally not true, except to use their superior empathy and body-language reading skills. If women don't follow the unwritten rules of business - they'll fail. Many men don't like the rules either, but they do abide by them as if they were written down. Perhaps when more women reach top management positions, some of the games played in business will become obsolete. In the meantime, women are encouraged to play the game within the existing rules - no matter how goofy and insane some of them appear. More on the rules of corporate gamesmanship in Chapter 3.

Step #23: Follow company rules the same as the men do

6. Most men stay clear of any women they perceive as a 'women's libber.' Aggressiveness in men is still tolerated but is absolutely forbidden in women.

Oh how true this is! Men and women have been putting up with aggressive male bosses for centuries. Are these bosses liked? Hardly - but they *are* obeyed. Now the female boss comes on the scene and foolishly tries to copy the behaviour of other aggressive male bosses. She's immediately ostracised, disciplined and/or demoted. This tactic simply doesn't work for women and soon won't for male managers either. More on this topic in Chapter 9.

Step #24: Act assertively – not aggressively and know the difference

Our next chapter will give you more insight into the 'Corporate Games played in Business.'

Chapter Three

Games played in business

It's been said that there are two ways to climb the corporate ladder - by climbing over other people or by developing your subordinates and letting them push *you* up. Obviously the second route is the most effective.

Unfortunately, most women don't get the chance to climb over anyone, because they seldom get the chance to put their feet on the first rung of the corporate ladder. Many have spent their lives working in support roles and don't know how to get out of that role into a supervisory or management position. No matter how hard they work, how dedicated and sincere they are in their wishes for a promotion - somehow they're consistently passed over.

This happens because most women don't realise that business is a game - the game of Corporate Politics. All profit-making companies follow the rules of this game. The most crucial rule of businesses is that they're out to earn money - not spend it. Everyone is expected to be dollar conscious. So, if you can think of something that will save your company money - you'll be listened to (provided you've got the facts to back up your idea) - and provided you present the idea in a way the people in charge can relate to. Remember not to use such phrases as: *'I feel ... I think ... or, I believe it will work.'* Give facts!

Don't go on and on about how much easier your way is going to make Tom's job. Instead, try to put a dollar value on how much money your company will save if your idea is adopted. For example, *'This will save our input workers' time and therefore save the company ... dollars per unit.'* Remember, if your idea is not accepted right away - don't give up – have Plan 'b' ready.

Because these rules of corporate gamesmanship are *unwritten*, women can take a lot of time to figure them out. Before most women step over the support-staff/executive boundary, most are unaware that on the other side of the barricade is a foreign country with customs, conditions, unwritten rules and ways of its own. The new female manager who doesn't realise that natives in this new world speak a different language, may wonder at first why she feels disoriented. Then she'll wonder how she can learn what she needs to know as quickly as possible, so she too can succeed.

Not only are there no road maps in business, there are no written rules of the game either (at least not any that women can see) but men seem to feel it instinctively and they act or react accordingly. If you ask men to explain what's happening or why they did what they did, they probably couldn't tell you what triggered their action, except that it felt right.

What do men know that women don't? How can rules be adhered to by men, if they're not written down? Well, it's because they've been taught these rules, bit by bit, through participation in competitive sports, through time spent in military services and through time spent working with, talking to and observing other men who know the ropes and being involved in 'the old boy's network.'.

Although most women feel that some of these corporate games are childish and that business should be conducted in a straightforward manner, they need to understand that these rules are rigidly adhered to by *successful* men and women. So they too will have to conform. Once they know the rules, they may not like them, but at least they'll know when they're breaking one. I broke a lot of rules as I climbed the corporate ladder, but didn't know I was breaking them. I felt very frustrated because I didn't know what I'd done wrong. Some women decide they just can't take the kind of game-playing that goes on in business and decide to opt out of it as I did and start their own companies. Learn more about whether you have what it takes to become an entrepreneur in Chapter 13.

Game playing in business

If you haven't read Betty Lehan Harragan's **Games Mother Never Taught You - Corporate Gamesmanship for Women**, - do so soon. It will open your eyes to what's really going on in business. For example: she explains that working is a game women never learned to play; that having women players on the team upsets the 'boys;' and it's important for women to learn to take charge and replace passivity with the habit of command.

When I finished reading Harragan's book, I felt very angry. I wasn't angry at her for identifying these games; I was angry that no one had explained them to me earlier. I suddenly realised why I had handled so many things incorrectly in the past. All the frustrations, barricades, what I felt were double-dealing, back-biting and buck passing I'd been subjected to in my climb up the ladder, now made sense. I'd always felt as if I was 'out of sync' in the business world and after talking to other women realised that many of them felt the same way too. I vowed to keep as many women as possible from making the same mistakes. By applying some of Harragan's insights to my own experience, I came up with the following sixteen rules.

RULE #1: Never undermine your immediate boss by going over his or her head to the next level with problems

I committed this *faux pas* over and over again and I just wasn't allowed to get away with it! After I understood that the hierarchies of business reflect the same type of chain-of-command you'd find in the military - I knew better.

All the rules in business are based on a combination of military regulations and rules of competitive sports. In sports and in the military, men learn that if their coach/sergeant tells them to do something, they'd better do it! And if their boss tells them to do something - they know they'd better do it. Your major function as an employee - is to make your boss look good. On the other hand, your supervisor's major function is to give you the necessary tools so you can do your own job properly.

If you go above your boss's head to her boss and say, *'I don't like the way she's supervising me,'* her boss isn't likely to do anything. His or her attitude will be, *'I pay your supervisor to do her job, so do what she says!'* Once you understand that ultimately *they're* as responsible for your tasks being completed properly as you are - you'll understand why tasks should be done to please them.

The ultimate person of importance to you is your immediate supervisor *who has the power to promote, demote or fire you.* Your supervisor's boss won't step in on your behalf - that's just not supposed to be done in business. I can't tell you how many times I went over my boss's head (especially if I thought he was incompetent) trying to get someone - anyone - to *'listen to some sense.'* It didn't seem possible to me that businesses would let someone be in a position of power with so little knowledge. I felt it was my obligation to pass on my brilliant ideas to my boss's boss, if my boss wouldn't listen to them. I was wrong! His boss didn't dare listen to me or he'd undermine the whole hierarchal system!

Recruits in the military learn that their senior officer is entitled to their respect and unquestioned obedience. This deference is given *solely* on the merit and importance of their rank. This means, no matter how incompetent the person is you're still expected to show respect! I couldn't - and still can't understand this tradition. If my boss was incompetent, I found it impossible to work for him or her. You may shake your head and say, *'I can't handle that rule either.'* That's unfortunate, because you'll have to abide by it. No more going over your boss's head! You may gain a small victory by identifying your boss's weaknesses, but in the long run you'll just set yourself up to fail.

The only exception to this rule is if the supervisor's actions are affecting several employees. Make every effort to settle the problem with your boss *before* taking this drastic step. Then (and only then) should you consider going above your boss's head to his or her superior or speak to a member of your Human Resources Department. If all the employees decide to bite the bullet and complain about their supervisor - make sure *everyone* involved has put down (in writing) their specific complaints, the repercussions because of the supervisor's actions and their perceived solutions to those complaints.

By putting their complaints down in writing you'll identify anyone in the group who will likely decide to renege at the last minute. Know that if they refuse to put their complaints in writing - they'll likely back down at the meeting as well. So know what kind of back-up you'll receive from the rest of the staff *before* you complain to anyone. Don't be left out on a limb by your more passive colleagues!

If it's just you who's affected by the supervisor and you've tried everything you can think of to improve your situation - you have three choices:

1. Put up with the situation as long as you can (Possibly until you're ready for the next promotion).
2. Make a lateral move to another department.
3. Get out as quickly as you can (move to another company).

If you decide to take a lateral move to another department, the position will most likely be in another specialty area. Suppose you want to stay in your original specialty area? You can get back to it by doing the following:

Work towards a promotion in your new department (which will likely make you a peer of your former boss); then, when an opportunity arises, apply for a promotion in your original specialty (making you your former boss's boss). Now guess who has control? Your former boss is not likely to get there before you, if s/he's as poor a supervisor as you believe.

RULE #2: Do only your job and its duties - no one else's

Normally, if companies hire you to do a job, they expect you do that job and nothing else. Catch yourself if you're slipping into someone else's area of responsibility. When women make this blunder male peers might comment, *'Don't help me, when I don't ask you to help me!'* Most women who have worked at home for a few years come back into the work force with the same attitude towards work as they had at home. If they see a job that needs doing - they simply roll up their sleeves and do it. That doesn't work in the business world unless you're invited to provide the help. Do your job and no one else's, no matter how much you're tempted to pitch in. When all your work is done (and only then) *offer* to help another worker - but finish *your* work first.

An example of this is: Denise's job was to process reports. She found she spent half her time correcting mistakes she found on the documents. What should Denise have done with those reports? She should have sent them back to the person who made the mistakes. Whose job was she doing? Who looked good and got the credit because the reports were done correctly; - the person who prepared the reports - not Denise. Who looked bad because she isn't getting her own work done? Denise.

Denise explained that she didn't want the other person to look bad, so she helped her out. If the errors were minor, requiring only small corrections, of course she should have made them, but she shouldn't have been spending her valuable time correcting someone else's major blunders. As well, she would have been blamed if she had made changes that turned out to be incorrect.

51

RULE #3: Demonstrate respect - and avoid showing disrespect towards your boss

Politicking, apple polishing, brown nosing and bootlicking - they're all the same thing. Such as:

Having your boss and his or her spouse over for dinner or taking them out for dinner; currying favour by giving senior staff free tickets to sporting activities;

Or doing anything underhanded to make you look good in the eyes of your boss.

Many people look for their boss's 'hot button' and push it. They spend time analysing what they can do to get on his or her right side. This has nothing to do with doing a good job; it's far more manipulative than that. If I were a boss and saw this going on, my respect for the person using these tactics would diminish. They certainly wouldn't get any 'Brownie Points' from me. To many women this is dishonest and underhanded and they refuse to take part in it.

They see their male colleague outside his boss's office preening before he goes in, showing respect, even deference to the supervisor. Women can't understand why the colleague puts on the show, when they know he hates his boss with a passion, believes he's an absolute idiot and certainly doesn't respect him. Women are more honest about this and it causes a lot of waves in business. Employees are expected to show respect to their bosses - whether they think they deserve it or not. If you really want to succeed, you're at least going to have to pretend to like your boss. You may decide to opt out of this game, but when you break this rule, at least you'll now know you're breaking it. Instead of politicking, apple polishing, brown nosing and bootlicking, concentrate your efforts on doing a good job - which will in turn make your boss look good.

RULE #4: Be wary of a promotion that's been offered to you, that has already been turned down by a man

You might initially say, *'How wonderful - I've been offered a promotion!'* Before accepting the position, stop and ask yourself why George didn't take it when it was offered to him. Talk to George and find out why *he* didn't take it. You might find there's something really wrong with the position. Maybe that job's going to be obsolete in six month's time or perhaps the boss you would report to is impossible to work for. George knows something you don't - so you owe it to yourself to ask him about it *before* accepting the position.

Have you ever taken a similar position, where you'd been set up to fail and didn't even know it? If you're offered any job and have reservations about it, ask for more time before making your decision. Then investigate. In the above example, it's possible that George had his eye on another job and your worries were unfounded - but do check things out.

RULE #5: Don't accept more and more responsibilities. Know your limits!

This one is a major failing of women. Some men fall into this trap, but it's mainly women who do it. Picture a woman at a desk with mounds and mounds of work on it and more and more keeps coming in. She remains going at top speed - but no matter how hard she works - she never gets to the bottom of the pile. How frustrating!

This is where good time management comes in. She needs to take a course in time management so she'll be able to set priorities. In time management courses, she'll be taught how to identify the rush jobs that have to be done right away, the jobs that have to be done that day and those that can be put off until tomorrow. The first ones she tackles, of course are the rush jobs. These tasks are examined and she decides which one of them has top priority, second priority, third priority, etc. The other two groups of tasks she puts into folders or baskets, preferably in another part of her work station so they won't cause her to be distracted. Then she'll determine how much time it will take to complete the tasks that need to be done that day. If she realises at this point that she can't handle all the tasks - it's time to speak to her boss and ask his or her opinion.

Because she's now on top of what she *can* do that day, she'll know what to say when extra tasks are dumped on her desk. She'll be able to say, *'I'd be happy to do that, but I don't have time to do that and the Miller report.'* Or, *'Does this take precedence over the rush job you gave me this morning?'* This leaves the decision up to the person giving her the work. Or she could say, *'I'm sure you want this task professionally done, but if I'm going to do both assignments in that space of time, I don't think my work will have the quality you want. Do they both have to be completed by noon?'* The supervisor then makes the choice, not her. This will make her boss realise she's organised enough to know when she's in over her head.

Some superiors keep giving more and more tasks until the employee complains and asks for a raise. Then the supervisor explains his or her displeasure at the quality of work the employee's been producing. Management's game is to get as much work as possible for no additional pay. Watch the men; for every new responsibility they accept, there's normally a salary increment - so keep track of your new duties and bring them up at performance appraisal time.

If you work for several bosses and find you're getting bogged down by too many tasks, advise them that you can't do all the jobs they want completed today and ask which ones can be left until tomorrow. Know ahead of time what you **can** do within the usual business hours of your firm (don't add overtime as part of your regular day).

Supervisors can help by placing small coloured labels on the work they give out, so their staff will know immediately which items are of top priority. Red is suggested for *'urgent'* (must be attended to immediately); yellow for *'must be done today;'* and green for *'can wait until tomorrow.'* The supervisor would add a date and time to the tags - especially deadlines for urgent 'red' items. This can also be done with e-mail assignments.

When planning your day, don't plan every minute of it. There are bound to be interruptions and crises. It's a good idea to keep track of the interruptions and crises you normally handle in a week. That way, you'll have a better idea how much time you *really* do have for planned work and can respond better to work overloads.

If you don't practice time management and go on the way you are, you'll probably keep going faster and faster, but what will you end up doing? Making mistake after mistake. Understandably, your manager can't be blamed if he believes, *'She can't even handle the position she's in, so how can she expect me to promote her?'* If you try to cram in all those duties, something's bound to happen to your accuracy rate.

RULE #6: Understand the company hierarchy

The office hierarchy (that is, the various ranks of employees) is usually defined on organisational charts. Have you seen the organisational charts for your company or at least your branch or department? If you haven't, locate one, so you can see how your position fits in. The charts can also show you how to get where you want to go within your company. You'll be able to identify the 'pecking order' and the status of each position.

These lines to the top are important for your future promotions. Although most lines appear to look progressive, if you check them carefully, only certain ones lead to top positions. You'll notice that nowhere on the organisational chart are clerical or secretarial positions shown, except as an adjunct to (or dotted line to) another position with little or no promotional opportunity.

The title *'assistant to'* doesn't necessarily mean that you're in line for the position you're the assistant to. Nor does the title 'office manager' always make you a manager on your way up the ladder. This too can be a dead-end position. Check things out before you choose a position with this title to see where the next step will lead you. These two positions could be compared to those of non-commissioned officers in the army. You'll seldom be given the chance to step on the first rung of the ladder, unless you obtain the same qualifications as the 'commissioned officers.' (This may require additional training or education.)

Line Positions

There are certain types of jobs that lead to the very top of the ladder. Any operations job that involves the production of goods or services or the selling of those goods or services will get you there. These line positions bring money *into* the company. These are in:

1. Marketing (determining through surveys and research who and where the target markets should be);
2. Sales (going to the target markets and selling the product or service to clients);
3. Engineering and technology;

55

4. Production (making the product or whatever the company sells);
5. Contract administration (making a contract to sell or service a client and following the product or service through credit checks, production, quality control, delivery, accounts receivable and accounts payable);
6. Research and design (finding new products the company can market. For instance, *'We're making this kind of product. How can we change it to succeed in another target market?'*

Staff or Service Positions

Staff or service positions, on the other hand, *cost* the company money to maintain. Keep in mind, that during a recession, staff positions will be eliminated before line positions are touched. Managers in staff or service positions seldom make policy decisions. They include positions in:

1. Purchasing (buying goods from other companies);
2. Data processing and computers;
3. Accounting;
4. Advertising;
5. Research (analyse why a product isn't working, rather than investigating new ones);
6. Traffic;
7. Billing;
8. Industrial relations or human resources
9. Medical services;
10. Legal services;
11. Public relations;
12. Credit services.

You'll notice that women fill many of these positions, but few of the line positions. If you're offered two positions at the same time, think carefully about which one is really the best for you. Let's say one is a promotion to a supervisory position (at a higher salary) within a staff department where you now work; the second is a lateral position (the job offers the same pay as you're getting now) but it's in a line position. Which one should you take?

After reading the preceding explanation, you're probably tempted to say 'yes' to the lateral line position. But, there's a further point to be made. Upon closer investigation, you discover the boss you would report to in the line position is one of the 'incompetents' we discussed earlier. In that case, it would probably be better to get a promotion in your staff department and eventually try to land a position above the 'incompetent.' You might also discover that you'll have less chance of obtaining a supervisory position in a line department, so you'll be ahead, if you obtain supervisory experience in a staff position.

Investigate all new positions thoroughly and weigh all the facts. Keep up-to-date on what's happening in the line department of your choice and when the timing's right - move in. Don't jump at the first supervisory position that's open - weigh all the factors. It could be that you're in a position close to the top of your present department, so a move to the lateral line position might be a better move for you.

If you really want to forge ahead fast, work for a medium-sized company. There are fewer people to climb over, for one thing. However, the smaller staff means you'll have to be more diversified. There's also more development of existing staff through necessity, rather than choice.

On the other hand, if you really want to know the most up-to-date method of doing something - work for a large progressive-thinking company. Their departments are normally broken down into more specific areas. To give you an example of this: in human resources I had to learn how to classify positions, so I worked full-time as a classification officer for a large company and stayed there until I mastered it. Then I went on to learn about recruitment, performance appraisals, company benefits, exit interviews, training etc. until I was truly a human resources generalist. Only then did I have the diversified experience that smaller companies were looking for.

RULE #7: Diversify your experience

It's important in business to have experience in as many areas as you can - both line and staff. But remember; always guide yourself into positions that lead you to where you want to go. Before accepting any new appointment, ask yourself whether it's helping you get where you ultimately want to be or whether you're just floating and accepting whatever comes along. Become a specialist in at least one area and keep your eyes open for what's going on in your company so you can pounce on opportunities as they arise.

RULE #8: Don't slip into careless work habits

If you're bored to tears with your job, you may find you do sloppy, careless work, paying little attention to detail and deadlines. If so, you're sabotaging yourself. You can't possibly be considered for a promotion when you're showing your superiors that you aren't ready for one. You can't blame them. Don't put yourself into this 'Catch 22' situation.

RULE #9: Beware of the manager who allows subordinates to by-pass you

Be alert for the male manager who appoints you as supervisor but, under the guise of 'helping' you, allows subordinates to by-pass you to obtain help directly from him. Your boss knows he's breaking a rule of the game and he wouldn't consider doing so with a male supervisor. Don't allow this to continue. Bring the matter to his attention and show him how he's undermining your control. Ask that he send the subordinates back to you to deal with their problems. Only involve your boss when the situation warrants it.

Other managers delegate tasks to your staff without letting you know. If they were following the proper chain of command, they would give the task to you to delegate downwards. Again, talk to your manager about the difficulties this is causing you by unfairly distributing the work-load amongst your staff.

RULE #10: Learn military tactics

In the military, there are commissioned officers, non-commissioned officers and privates. Privates are part of the rank and file - ordinary soldiers without rank. They're at the bottom, below non-commissioned officers (which include sergeants and warrant officers). Commissioned officers are those ranks above warrant officer. In business there's a very similar structure. Privates are clerical, secretarial and support staff. Non-commissioned officers are foremen and supervisors. Commissioned officers are managers and executives.

All of these groups operate according to certain *traditions* - sets of rules, many of which are unwritten. Traditions often don't make sense, but traditional ways of doing things can often be the hardest to change. (*'It's always been done this way!'*)

Very few privates ever manage to rise even to non-commissioned officers level and very few clerks and personal assistants make it to supervisory or management levels. It's time to leave this tradition behind. Following the unwritten rules will enable women to do so.

RULE #11: Understand the relevance of team sports in the workplace

It's not enough to be aware of the military code that prevails in business. You must also understand how the code of competitive team sports shapes corporate activity. Most men understand team sports and enjoy a competitive atmosphere. The woman who grows up participating in competitive *team* sports is very lucky. Most women have spent their time competing against themselves. I spent six years of my life competing in competitive sports, but in swimming (an individual, rather than a team sport such as soccer). I was competing against myself, rather than belonging to a team that competes against other teams. It took me many years to realise I lacked an understanding of the rules of teamwork.

In talking with managers about how effective women were as team members, most related that women performed better when working by themselves. They were not as productive as men when involved in team projects and seemed to lack the 'team spirit' necessary for success.

When women rise to the management level, they must have *'the team spirit'* and work well with their male peers. They need to keep in mind that the whole team depends on them to do their work as part of a coordinated effort. Some women neglect to check with their co-workers to see if there have been any major changes or if they can supply some essential information needed to complete the project.

RULE #12: Remember that team players conform to the rules, not the rules to the players

Just as players have to conform to the rules of football, basketball and baseball, women have to conform to the rules of the game in business. *They* have to conform to the established rules of the game of business and cannot expect the rules to be adjusted to suit them (at least not yet). Women are slowly, but surely making a difference as more of them obtain management and executive positions, but it will be a while before the rules change significantly. In the meantime, if a player breaks the rules, s/he is penalised or held back.

What would likely happen if you were the only woman in a team of men and you let them see that you were a lot better than they? You'll be booted out. You can be a bit better, but it had better not be too much better - or the others will sabotage your efforts. Then your manager will notice that you're not 'one of the team' and get rid of you - no matter how good you are! This was one of the major mistakes I made. At one point I was handling three people's jobs at one time. This became necessary when two men in my peer group (who did essentially the same work as I) were absent for three weeks. I was the only one left to handle the work. The job was there; it had to be done; I seemed the only one qualified to do it; so I simply did it. What a mistake! I should have thought of the repercussions to my co-workers and asked for help from people in another division. (In fact, I would have burned out by the fourth week if I'd kept going at that breakneck pace.)

It didn't help to have my boss mention my feat to my co-workers when they returned. I hadn't thought of how threatening this must have been to them. They were obviously anxious that their jobs might be eliminated if one person could handle the whole caseload. They were rightfully upset and eventually made things rather uncomfortable for me.

Ask yourself if you've done this in the past or (heaven forbid) if you're doing it right now. If so, stop trying to be so much better than your co-workers. Be a little bit better, so your boss notices; but for the most part, try to blend in with the rest of the team. This rule applies to both men and women. If you're at this stage and *that* good, it usually means you're ready for a promotion.

The phrase you may hear that tells you you're *not* blending in with the team is, *'You're making waves.'* If you hear someone *in authority* use that expression - be careful. You're stepping on somebody's toes. Stand back and look at what you're doing and whom you're offending.

Business Language

Military language is used in business. Terms such as boondocks, boonies, flak, formation, jock, rank and file, scuttle-butt (gossip), sick bay and the old favourite T.G.I.F. (Thank God It's Friday) - all came from the military. Sports lingo is everywhere in the business world too: (touch base, tackle the job, batting average, out in left field, coach, mate, disqualified player, jock, team player, rules of the game, front line, ball-park figure, college try, pinch hitter, end run, huddle, good sport and bench sitter).

Another of these terms is *'Play your position.'* If your boss ever uses this phrase, he's probably saying: *'Do your own job or else!'* To expand on sports analogy, he sees that your job was to play centre for that game, but you played defence and he wants to know why. Men seem to understand that they have to play their position and no one else's and wonder why women don't understand this rule.

In competitive sports, losing the 'game' (failure at something you attempt) is a sign that more practice is necessary. Men know this. However, women often feel they've failed at something and take this failure personally. Never accept defeat. Instead - come back fighting. To men, there's no disgrace in losing while you're trying, but there is, if you *'give up the game,'* which they think of as the *'sissy or girl's way.'*

RULE #13: Know the strengths of women in business and learn to use them efficiently

Do you know what advantages women have in business? It's been said that women are more flexible and can accept change more quickly and easily. Another advantage women appear to have is the ability to handle several things at one time. Because they've practiced organisational skills in a multi-faceted home setting, they're better able to juggle competing tasks (as long as they have an

61

organised boss who's not dumping all his or her excess information on their desks).

What other advantages do you think they have? Here are some that I believe women have, which you may never have thought of as advantages:

Language skills

Scientific studies have shown repeatedly that women have much better verbal skills (oral and written) than men. Because many women started out in secretarial or clerical positions, they've needed these skills to enable them to correct spelling, grammar and punctuation mistakes of their supervisors.

Communication skills

I talked about these earlier. They are women's superior ability to read body language and their capacity for empathy. Keep using these skills and improve them by practicing and reading about them. The better you read body language, the better you're going to be able to understand others. For example: Your boss walks in. You see by his body language that he's having a *bad day;* so you know you'd better act accordingly. This skill of reading non-verbal clues is invaluable when dealing with family, subordinates and co-workers. Body language very seldom lies. The spoken words of others should be disregarded if their body language is telling you something else.

The ability to understand what someone else is feeling (empathy) is also invaluable. But beware: this skill is only useful if you can avoid getting too involved. Don't take on others' sorrows and troubles as your own.

Intuition

Women call it intuition. Most men call it a 'gut reaction' or a 'hunch.' This can occur when you have the feeling that you really should - or should not - do something. More often than not, you can't put a finger on why you feel *that way,* but you'll seldom be able to do so.

I had intuition explained to me this way: When you get a flash of intuition, every single scrap of information in your sub-conscious brain is used to come up with the feeling. If you listen to your second idea (which is usually based on your conscious brain) you'll be using only a portion of all the information available to you. I like to compare our brains to computers. Your subconscious brain (hard drive) has a memory bank far superior to lower-grade software (your conscious brain). When you listen to your intuition, you're using a superior memory bank. If you listen to only your second idea, you're using a low grade or inferior memory bank.

Now, which one should you listen to? Of course! Listen to your intuition. When it tells you something - listen to it. It's seldom wrong. The only time I haven't listened to my intuition was when I took an instant dislike to someone. After standing back, I realised that this person physically resembled another person whom I disliked and distrusted. By turning off my intuitive feelings, I was able to learn that the person was okay.

I remember an incident when my intuition kicked in. While driving, I was passing some parked cars and thought I saw some movement in front of one of them, but as I came closer did not see anything. However, I felt the need to stop and check it out. What I found has haunted me for years – what I saw crawling out from behind the parked car (and would have been right in front of my wheels as I passed) was a baby crawling on the road. I put my emergency flashers on my car and tried to determine where the baby had come from. I followed the direction it had come from and saw a sidewalk leading to stairs and an open front door to a home. I picked up the baby and went to the door, rang the bell and was greeted by a young woman who stared at me holding her baby and asked, *'What are you doing with my baby?'*

I pointed to my car and told her the story. She thanked me profusely and promised that she would put a lock on the door so the baby could not sneak out again.

Creative Problem Solving

Many years ago, companies started using creative problem-solving techniques. A problem was defined to a group and they brainstormed to come up with as many workable solutions to their problem as possible. One of the rules of brainstorming is that you offer your ideas without censoring them. No matter how silly the idea appears, it should be offered, because it may in turn trigger a better suggestion from someone else in the group. Everyone in the room takes part and one person writes down the ideas.

In one company, this technique was moderately successful, until one day a manager who couldn't make it to a meeting, sent his personal assistant to take notes for him. Since everyone was expected to participate - she was asked to contribute as well. The managers couldn't believe the outcome - she came up with two of the four workable solutions! They couldn't understand why her answers were better than those of the professionals who understood all aspects of the problem.

At the next meeting they experimented. The managers brought their secretaries to the meeting. Again, most of the ideas came from the women. It seems that the women didn't censor their ideas as critically as men. The men generally questioned their ideas to see if they were good enough *before* submitting them to the group. They did this out of fear of looking silly or because they couldn't turn off their self-censoring mechanism that told them, *'That won't work.'*

In this case, the women had been told to let ideas flow unrestricted - so they did. They voiced any idea they could possibly think of. It didn't matter whether it was a good idea because they'd been told their ideas would be censored. Also, they were not as worried about looking silly. Many businesses now make sure half their participants at creative-problem-solving sessions are women.

Drive to Succeed

Many women coming back into the workforce for a second career have a tremendous drive to succeed perhaps because they feel their major role in life (as a homemaker and mother) is essentially over. They don't want to feel as if they're 'over the hill' or hate the emptiness in their lives. All the energy they once gave to homemaking and raising children is now expended towards getting ahead in business. This is especially true of women who hope to progress into management positions.

Because these women are 'fresh,' many have more stamina and enthusiasm than men and women who've been in the workforce for fifteen or twenty years. Some of those workers have hit a plateau and many have lost some of their momentum and zeal. The dynamism of these newcomers can be rather threatening to others whose momentum has stalled.

These men and women had this identical drive when they were twenty and first starting out, but they've forgotten the feeling. To keep interested and motivated, these workers should set new career goals for themselves that are more applicable to their current skills and abilities.

RULE #14 - Don't date workmates or clients

Can you identify some of the problems that could occur if you decided to date a co-worker, supervisor or a regular client of your company? Most women believe that this kind of arrangement is all right - that it doesn't affect their chances of succeeding. Occasionally it might work out, but the odds are that it won't. To be safe, stay clear of dating anyone you work with or have as a client. This is especially deadly if you work in the middle- or upper-management levels.

What causes most office romances? Proximity and availability. Think about the amount of time most husbands spend (awake) with their spouses? Married female employees spend just about the same length of time (often more) with male colleagues as they spend with their spouses. Single women with boyfriends, find the same thing. They must not let their hormones take over and should think of the consequences they'd face if the romance breaks up. Inevitably, it will be difficult for both of parties - but if one of them has to go - it will probably be the woman (who's likely in a lower-level position than the man). If neither of them goes, it will cause a serious strain on their relationship in the office and their colleagues will be watching for repercussions.

It's amazing how fast colleagues catch on to the 'office romance.' The couple may think they've pulled the wool over everyone's eyes, but their body language will probably give them away. This kind of romance can be even more tragic if the person is the woman's mentor (mentors are covered in Chapter 12).

RULE #15 - Your boss has the right to take credit for your ideas

Both women and men have been heard to say, *'I worked all week on that report and my boss took the credit for it. That's the last time he's going to do that to me!'* When your boss 'steals' and takes credit for your idea, you've made him look good. And he needs you to do this. If this bothers you, send your good ideas and suggestions to your boss in the form of an e-mail, asking his opinion about the merit of your ideas. Then it's in writing. Better yet - offer your suggestions at a meeting where others hear about your new idea.

According to the rules of the game, he has the *right* to steal your ideas and do it with a clear conscience. According to business rules, you (the subordinate) are there to make your supervisor look good. Most men and women dislike this rule, but the men abide by it. Your ideas become your boss's ideas and he's not breaking any rules by taking credit for them. The funny thing is that male supervisors don't feel they're doing anything wrong - because everybody does it. For instance, if you write a new policy and procedures manual for your department, your boss can take full credit for its contents even though you did all the work.

However, when you become a supervisor - try not to continue this practice. As I explain more fully in the chapter on supervisory skills (Chapter 8) it's a good idea for a supervisor to give credit where credit is due

RULE #16 - Learn to use logic instead of emotion

Men believe that the feminine trait of using emotions when making decisions is far inferior to their method of using 'logic.' However, many companies are spending a fortune pushing for better interpersonal skills. This suggests that they realise these 'female' traits have their merit. But while men are being encouraged to be less logical and more emotional, women are being encouraged to rely less on emotions when making decisions. So we're looking forward to a nice mixture of these qualities sometime in the future.

Although these sixteen rules cannot cover all of the games played in business, these are the ones I feel are most crucial for aspiring female supervisors, managers and executives to follow.

Chapter Four

Career goals

Career Planning

Some people believe a career is something that only professionals such as doctors and lawyers have. Not true. Everyone has a career and make many career decisions throughout their lifetime. But if making a career decision is normal, then why is it so difficult, confusing and over-whelming? Decisions such as which occupation to choose, what type of training or education to pursue or whether to change jobs, can be too harrowing for many. So they do nothing.

As a 34 year-old homemaker put it, *'After being out of the workforce for ten years, I'd like to go back - but my skills are outdated.'*

And a fifty-five-year-old senior manager laments, *'I was laid off after working for twenty years with the same company. At my age - how can I find another job?'*

The answer is - obtain career counselling. There are three terms used in career planning:

A *job* is a position with specific duties and responsibilities. For example: teaching year three at Hillside Primary School is a job.

An *occupation* is a group of similar jobs in society (teacher, engineer, etc.).

A *career* is the sum total of your work-related experience, including both paid and unpaid labour.

A job is what you do with your days
- a career is what you do with your life!

Work-related experience includes full- and part-time work, parenting and homemaking, volunteer and community work, hobbies and other leisure activities that may influence a person's work now or in the future. People may change jobs or even occupations, but each person has only *one* career.

If I were to ask you how many years the average woman worked outside her home either part-time or full-time - what would you answer? The average woman will spend approximately thirty-five years of her life working outside the home either part- or full-time (or all but ten years of her adult life before retirement). Shocking, isn't it! So if you're in a boring job now, ask yourself how many more years you have left to work in a job you hate. You have two distinct choices - stay and suffer or find something better. (By the way - it's forty-five years for men, but they seldom do all the 'volunteer' work that women do around the home.)

Working at a career you're suited for can be tremendously stimulating. The work generates its own momentum and you genuinely feel you're realising your dreams. Those in this category can't wait to get up in the morning. Mondays are exciting and they start the day running. With this attitude towards their work, they have a much better chance of progressing within the career they've chosen. The big question of course is how to find the career that suits them.

Have you set concrete career goals? Successful men and women have. From the time they're about eleven years of age; most boys have a good idea how to answer the question: *'What are you going to be when you grow up?'* Ask most girls that age the same question and they'll likely give you a blank look. Somehow, they don't think this is an important issue for women.

Usually these girls grow up having their parents set goals for them; later their goals are geared towards the needs of husbands and children, rather than to themselves and their own wants and needs. Women with this kind of background, find setting personal and career goals for themselves a big challenge. However, the positive results can make it well worth their effort.

Mid-life Career Changes

More and more people are making drastic career changes in mid-life. A mid-life career change occurs when you switch from an occupation you've been established in for a considerable length of time, to a completely different one. We *choose* some mid-life career changes - others are *forced* upon us. Making this change, often involves leaving an established position to go into an entry-level position, which may involve a significant loss in income and ego. The individual may need additional training before s/he can make the switch. Whenever possible - never leave one position without having another to go to.

More often than not, mid-life career changes affect others. We may be well established, with a network of relationships, commitments, responsibilities and obligations to family and work, so making a change of this kind is difficult and complicated. Our burning desire for change is mixed with guilt feelings that we're imposing our needs on our families. This may hold us back from making the necessary move. But you may feel that time is running out! It may be now or never - and every day you spend at your present job is one day less that you'll have to do what you really want to do. So panic starts setting in.

Mixed in with the guilt, are fears and doubts about making the change; feelings of frustration if you aren't working towards the change; feelings of uncertainty about whether to stay where you are; and hope about the promise of better things, if you go. Like all change, this type of move offers opportunities for self-fulfilment, challenge and personal satisfaction. But change of any kind also has a way of making us feel vulnerable and unsure of ourselves. Even the most self-assured people are shaken by change, so the support of family and friends becomes more important - so seek their support during your career changes. If you feel your own self-esteem is the problem, Chapter 9 will help you feel good about yourself and improve your self-confidence during stressful times such as this.

The importance of setting career goals

When I was working as a Human Resources Manager, a young woman came to me and explained that she was at the top of her clerical level and wanted to know what promotional opportunities were available in our company. I asked her where *she* wanted to go - what occupation *she* had chosen. She replied, *'I don't really care what job I get, as long as it's a promotion and pays me more money.'*

I explained to her that she had gone as far as she could go as a generalist (and in the clerical field at that) - that now she'd have to specialise. She still didn't appear to understand what I meant, so I suggested careers in marketing, computers, human resources, accounting, sales, operations or production. She just shrugged her shoulders and repeated her original statement about money.

She failed to understand that companies don't just offer jobs to people; the applicant needs to prove she has done something to earn herself the promotion. Instead of preparing herself for promotional opportunities - she expected her company to 'find' the opportunities for her. For instance, if she wanted eventually to become a purchasing manager, she should have taken related courses in the evening so she'd be ready for the next junior buyer's position available in her company.

I sent her away to investigate where she wanted to use her talents and abilities - but never heard from her again; it was too much trouble. This was a shame; because I had several positions (junior buyer, marketing representative, transportation specialist) that I could have offered her if she had taken the time to choose her career path.

Determining your transferrable skills

The first step in the career choice area is to determine your transferrable skills. Transferrable skills (supervisory skills, interpersonal skills, accounting knowledge, aptitude with figures, scheduling skills, etc.) are those skills that can be taken from one occupational field into another. It's a good idea to ask your close friends and relatives to help you with this set of questions. They may see qualities in you that you've overlooked. Complete the following to determine some of your transferrable skills:

Decide whether you:

> **Can do well**
> **Can do**
> **Would like to do well**
> **Can't do well**
> **Not interested**

1. Moving your body

a) USING MOTOR CO-ORDINATION - Being well coordinated when moving different parts of your body.

b) ACTING QUICKLY - Doing something fast when necessary.

c) USING STAMINA - Continually doing physically tiring work without becoming exhausted.

d) USING STRENGTH - Doing heavy work - lifting, pulling or carrying heavy things.

2. Paying attention to detail

a) FOLLOWING PROCEDURES - Doing things exactly as directed. Completing tasks at the right time and in the right order.

b) VERIFYING - Checking numbers or written materials to make sure they're right. Checking the work of others.

c) RECORD KEEPING - Maintaining written records of money, objects, merchandise, things or facts.

d) SORTING - Sorting things in the right order. Putting things in the correct place or category.

3. Using your hands

a) USING YOUR FINGERS - Being exact when you use your fingers to hold or move things.

b) OPERATING - Controlling, guiding or otherwise running tools, machines, vehicles, electronic devices or equipment.

c) ASSEMBLING - Putting things together.

d) ADJUSTING - Changing the settings on machines, devices, musical instruments or electrical equipment to improve their performance.

e) BUILDING/CONSTRUCTING - Using tools/equipment to build or construct objects, buildings or structures.

f) FIXING/REPAIRING - Fixing equipment, tools, machinery, appliances, etc.

4. Leading others

a) MAKING DECISIONS - Choosing an action and accepting responsibility for the consequences.

b) DIRECTING/SUPERVISING - Overseeing or managing the work of others and accepting responsibility for their performance.

c) INITIATING - Taking the first step. Getting things started.

d) CONFRONTING - Telling others something that they don't want to hear about their behaviour, habits, etc.
e) PLANNING - Developing projects or ideas through systematic preparation and deciding in which order and at what time events will occur.
f) ORGANISING - Coordinating the people and resources necessary to put a plan into effect.

5. Using numbers

a) COUNTING - Determining how many items there are in one group.
b) CALCULATING - Using basic arithmetic; adding, subtracting, multiplying and dividing.
c) MEASURING - Using tools or equipment to determine length, angle, volume or weight.
d) ESTIMATING - Judging the cost or size of things. Predicting the outcome of an arithmetic problem before it's calculated.
e) BUDGETING - Planning exactly how you will spend money. Deciding what merchandise to buy and how much to spend or how to get the work done at the lowest cost.
f) USING NUMERICAL REASONING - Understanding how to work with numbers or statistics. Using numbers to solve problems. Knowing how to read data and interpret statistics.

6. Using your senses

a) USING SOUND DISCRIMINATION - Hearing slight differences in sound.
b) USING COLOUR DISCRIMINATION - Seeing small differences in colours.
c) USING SHAPE DISCRIMINATION - Seeing small differences in shapes and sizes, observing how things are alike or different.
d) USING DEPTH PERCEPTION - Accurately judging distance, judging how far away or apart things are.

7. Being helpful

a) SERVING - Caring, doing things for others, providing a service upon request or when others are in need.
b) TREATING - Performing a treatment to relieve a person's physical or psychological problems.

c) CO-OPERATING - Working together with others to reach a common goal; working as part of a team to complete tasks.

d) ADVISING/COUNSELLING - Helping others cope with their personal / emotional / educational / family / career concerns by providing information or suggesting ways to solve their problems.

e) TEACHING/TRAINING - Helping others learn how to do or understand something.

8. Being creative

a) VISUALISING/IMAGINING - Being able to form a mental image of concepts, objects, forms, drawings, models blueprints, etc.

b) CREATING/INVENTING - Originating new ideas or inventing new ways of doing things.

c) DESIGNING/DISPLAYING - Dealing creatively with spaces, products, objects, colours or images.

d) PERFORMING/ENTERTAINING - Getting up in front of an audience or camera to entertain.

e) IMPROVISING/EXPERIMENTING/ADAPTING - Making changes or modifications to get the job done. Finding new and creative ways to accomplish tasks.

f) DRAWING/PAINTING/SCULPTING - Conveying feelings or thoughts through works of art.

g) WRITING/PLAYWRITING/COMPOSING - Creating new and original materials to entertain or amuse.

9. Using logical thinking

a) INVESTIGATING/RESEARCHING - Gathering information in an organised way in order to establish certain facts or principles.

b) ANALYSING - Breaking a problem into its parts so that each part can be dealt with separately.

c) SYNTHESISING - Putting facts and ideas together in new and creative ways - finding new ways to look at problems or do things, creating new ideas by putting old ideas together in a new way.

73

10. Communicating with others

a) READING - Getting information from written materials. Following written instruction on what to do or how to operate something.

b) WRITING - Using good grammar to make sentences and paragraphs that make sense. Being able to express oneself and explain things in writing.

c) TALKING - Finding it easy to talk to strangers in ordinary conversation settings.

d) SPEAKING - In front of a group or audience.

e) LISTENING - Listening carefully to whatever the other person is saying and responding appropriately.

f) QUESTIONING - Asking the right questions to get useful information from others or to help them gain insight.

g) NEGOTIATING - Bargaining with others to solve a problem or reach an agreement.

h) READING BODY LANGUAGE - Understanding what a person is saying non-verbally.

i) EXPLAINING - Being careful and clear when you're telling people about things, so that they can understand you quickly and easily.

j) PERSUADING - Convincing others to do what you want.

Career Changes

One woman, who came to me for career counselling was working as a nursing supervisor, but because she now had a young family, found she couldn't adapt to shift work. She was worried that she wouldn't be able to find work in any other occupation. I helped her determine what her transferrable skills were. These consisted of such things as:

- An ability to supervise others;
- A knowledge of scheduling (to give patients medication etc);
- Highly honed interpersonal skills to deal with all kinds of people from uppity doctors to cranky patients;
- The ability to keep meticulously detailed reports;
- Able to remain calm in emergencies;
- Was physically fit; and
- Able to make decisions quickly.

These were talents that could be useful in many occupations. She just had to find out which occupation she wanted to try.

She admitted that one of her passions was ladies' fashions. After examining her transferrable skills, I advised her that if she obtained the necessary retail training, her existing transferrable skills could be used as follows:

- A knowledge of scheduling (only she'd be scheduling buying of stock);
- An ability to supervise others;
- Highly honed interpersonal skills to deal with all kinds of people from upset clients to cranky staff;
- The ability to keep meticulously detailed reports (stock records, sales, bookkeeping);
- Able to remain calm in emergencies (possible robbery or fire);
- Was physically fit (would be on her feet most of the day); and
- Able to make decisions quickly (when buying stock, marking-down merchandise).

She'd likely have little trouble obtaining a position in a ladies' fashion shop. She decided to obtain the retail training and eventually worked her way up to the position of regional manager of an international ladies fashion outlet. Her skills as a nursing supervisor prepared her very well for her new career. She just had to fill in the gaps with relevant training.

In the past, I've had the opportunity of helping many men and women with career counselling. One fellow (a mechanical engineer) had been very successful in his field, but he had a nervous breakdown at the age of forty. He had met his goals, but suddenly realised he didn't like what he had become or what he was doing! Unfortunately, his father and brother were mechanical engineers, so he had decided to follow their lead.

When asked what he would rather be doing - he replied, *'You'll think I'm nuts, because I couldn't possibly earn enough doing what I want to do.'* He went on to explain, *'I was walking through the major appliance section of a department store and found myself explaining to a couple the ins and outs of the refrigerator they were looking at. The salesman didn't seem to be able to answer their technical questions and it felt great that I could help them understand how everything worked. But I could never earn as much money as a refrigerator salesman as I do at my existing job.'*

It turned out that he was so close to his problem; he couldn't see that he would be invaluable to many companies. I had interviewed hundreds of engineers and knew he had a unique talent. Many engineers admit they have trouble communicating their ideas either orally or in writing, but this man's communication skills were exceptional. I suggested he contact several firms that produce and sell technically difficult mechanical products to ask them if they required a sales-person with his background. He did so and within a week he received five job offers.

Like many people who come for career counselling, he had no perspective on his situation, so couldn't see his own talents. (Try holding your hand an inch or two in front of your face. You can't see it clearly, can you? It's too close.) In career counselling, the counsellor stands back far enough to see things that the individuals can't see for themselves.

Another client, a forty-year-old woman, consulted me when she was thinking about starting a second career. She wanted to be an accountant, but she thought she was *'over the hill and too old to learn.'* I asked her how many years she expected to work until retirement. After doing some calculations, *'Twenty-five years,'* she said. Then I asked her my standard question: *'Do you want to stay in a low-level, boring job until then or would you rather do what* you *want to do?'* She agreed that she wanted to change but still had serious reservations.

'It will take me four years of university to get the degree I need.' I asked her to consider how many years she would still be working after obtaining her degree. *'Twenty-one years.'* was her reply. I asked her if the opportunity to spend twenty-one years of her life doing what she wanted to do would make the sacrifice worthwhile. Her affirmative answer started her on the road to serious career planning.

At any age, you should be thinking about this - especially if you've been marking time in a job you dislike. Being successful in your chosen career does take time, energy dedication and effort. Don't go into something unless you really want to make a go of it. There's too much competition out there - people who know where they want to go and how they're going to get there. And never 'put your eggs in one basket.' Always have alternative occupations you could investigate, should the economy or technology make your existing occupation redundant.

Think about the successful people you know. Did they put a lot of time, energy, effort and dedication into getting where they wanted to go? You'll probably find they did, because success doesn't come without all of those things and you must be willing to do so as well.

Freedom from the pink-collar ghetto

Here's how you can move up from a pink-collar position in a company into a supervisory position:

Step 1. Decide *where* you want to go. Then investigate *how* you can get there. Is it through on-the-job training or will you require formal education and/or training? Once you find out, obtain that training, possibly while working at a junior-level position in the field of your choice. Go through the goal-setting process (described later in this chapter).

Step 2. Document every task you do in your present position. Determine whether you're doing an important part of your boss's job. Look for those tasks that require independent action and/or decision-making on your part. If you can identify the decisions you now make, you may be able to convince your employer that you're capable of making more major ones, but you'll just be using different kinds of data. Look for duties in which your judgment was crucial to the outcome of a task. Look for clear-cut areas of responsibility, authority and accountability. In other words, look for things you do on a regular basis where *you* decide the outcome. These are the skills management requires and you'll be well paid for using them.

Step 3. Obtain career counselling so you can identify your transferrable skills and learn about other occupational options that would use your existing skills and abilities.

Step 4. Ask your boss if your talents could be utilised in other areas of his or her department. Ask to see the company organisational charts, to identify other types of career paths. If necessary, explain that you're willing to take a cut in salary to start you on your chosen

77

career path. (Even a junior position - as long as it has a toehold on the bottom rung of the promotional ladder - is better than a clerical one.)

If your boss doesn't respond, talk to a member of your Human Resources Department. Identify the decision-making qualities you've developed and what specialty you'd like to get into. Ask them to let you know about any positions that come up that might utilise your qualifications.

As a backup, watch for job postings on the company bulletin board and be sure to apply for positions you believe you can handle. Have the Human Resources Department explain why you weren't suitable for the vacancies you apply for. They'll explain where you need to improve your qualifications. Then do so.

Step 5. Talk with someone in a high position who's eager to see women progress in business and ask his or her advice on what kinds of experience or education you're lacking to get where you want to go.

Step 6. When responding to ads, stay clear of those that describe the position or the candidate with words such as *skills, right arm, high-class, bright, achiever, hard working, support services, assistant to, pleasant working conditions,* etc. These denote lower-level positions. Watch instead for words such as *self-starter, career-oriented, challenging position,* etc. More senior positions will quote an annual, rather than hourly, weekly or monthly salary.

Step 7. Ask senior women in your company (and others) to help you reach your goal. Most of them will be glad to help you. Ask them how they got where they are and the route they took to get there.

Choosing a professional career counsellor

If you require help in career counselling, how do you select good professional help? This is a very difficult question to answer, because there are no officially accepted professional standards for most career counsellors. Unfortunately, not all career counsellors are equipped to help you, nor do many of them have the background to advise you fully. To choose a good counsellor, spend time researching these questions:

78

- What background and professional training does this person have? Post-secondary training in vocational guidance (not just personnel counselling) is a good starting point. In addition, at least a year of work experience in an appropriate setting (i.e.: educational institution, government agency) would teach this person to apply his or her learning in real-life situations.

- What do this person's past clients have to say about his or her career counselling experience? Legitimate agencies and/or private career counsellors will supply a list of past clients (with their permission) for references.

- How flexible is the person's approach to career planning? Promoting only one route to career satisfaction or a very narrow selection of tests and tools could be a sign of professional rigidity or incompetence.

- Does this person appear knowledgeable and current about today's labour market? The only way a prospective career planner can be assured of finding a *good* career counsellor is to learn the basics of career planning (by reading any of a number of excellent career - planning books available from colleges, universities and government agencies) and to be willing to ask why the counsellor is suggesting certain activities or exercises. Shop around until you feel right about the counsellor's personal style and attitude.

- Knowledgeable career counsellors will know what qualifications are required for different positions and where this training can be obtained through full-time study at a college or university, evening or correspondence courses. Counsellors should also know which companies provide on-the-job training.

Tests and Tools

There are many tests and tools that can be used in the first phase of the career counselling process to gather information about your aptitudes, abilities and preferences. These include such things as:

Aptitude tests, which try to predict how you would do in certain ability areas (i.e.: reasoning, verbal and perceptual).

Interest tests, which try to measure what you like to do, based on your past experiences and your personality (i.e.: working with tools, versus working with people).

Values inventories, which help clarify and then rank your life and career values (i.e.: the kind of work setting you want, the amount of energy you want to put into your work).

Skills inventories, which try to assist you to clarify and rank the work-related skills you already have. The focus is usually on transferrable skills that are useful in more than one occupational setting (i.e.: communication skills, budgeting).

Personality tests, which try to assess and categorise your over-all personal characteristics. This is the most nebulous kind of test and most open to bias on the part of a counsellor. These tests usually must be administered, scored and interpreted by a testing specialist or trained psychologist. Trained professionals will be able to determine which tests show sex biases in their questions. Sex bias is defined as any factor that might influence a person to limit - or might cause others to limit - his or her considerations of a career, solely on the basis of gender. The perceptions of both client and counsellor have to be unbiased.

If used carefully, standardised vocational tests can expand the choices, even if the tests contain some degree of sex bias, provided the counsellor is aware of the problems in the test. For example, if the pronoun *'he'* is used or if such terms as *'salesman, policeman,'* etc., consistently appear - the test is probably biased and will not give a correct reading unless the counsellor is aware of the implications of the testing device.

The use of *'she'* when referring to such traditionally female occupations as personal assistant or nurse is another such indication. The counsellor's own personal beliefs also influence the testing process and must be taken into account. If the counsellor appears to show bias against women - find another counsellor.

For those contemplating a change in occupation, obtain help in preparing your resume. Unless you really know how to put a resume together, your qualifications may not appear to your best advantage. On average, more than 100 people apply for every advertised position - often more. The only thing that sells your unique talents (and gets you in the door for an interview) is your resume - so it's *got* to be good. I'm an advocate of the 'custom-made' resume (writing a separate resume for every job you apply for).

Read the advertisement carefully to determine what the company is looking for. If the ad asks for a self-starter, you'd better give reasons why you *are* a self-starter. Do the same for every requirement or qualification asked for. Give the employer exactly what s/he wants (but don't lie).

Career-planning information

There are six major steps in planning a career:

1. Analyse what you like to do. You know what you like to do. Your career should allow you do to as many of those things as possible. You should feel as if you're cheating when you put your hand out for your paycheque because you're enjoying yourself so much.
2. Analyse what you do well. Most people have difficulty identifying what they do well. If you have trouble with this, you might ask a friend to help you identify those areas. Identify your transferrable skills. Complete the questionnaire in this chapter
3. Match your interests and abilities to a job. The things you like to do are your interests. The things you can do well are your abilities. Write down these interests and abilities. You're now in a position to start your research. Try to see your interests in terms of the work world. What work do you see others doing that really interests you? The best source of information about any career is the person working in the job. Ask them if they're willing to answer some questions relating to their positions.

   You'll find most people love talking about their jobs and will be honest about the things they like and dislike about their occupations.

   If you don't know someone in the occupation, contact the heads of the Human Resources Departments of companies that employ people in these occupations. See if they can arrange for you to talk to some of their employees. Or you might work part-time in a position in this occupation to learn about it first-hand.

Explore many occupations to determine what *you* like or dislike about them. Make notes of your observations for future reference. Read about what other people are doing. Would you like to do similar kinds of work? Even the want ads in newspapers can give you ideas about the kinds of jobs available in fields that appeal to you.

When assessing these occupations, there are three key questions you should try to answer:

    a. What qualifications are required for this job?
    b. Would I like to work in that kind of job?
    c. What promotional opportunities does the job offer?

4.   Decide what you want from work.
Once you understand what you like to do, what you do well and what types of occupations are suited to both your interests and abilities – consider the following questions, to help you determine what you want from your work:

    a) What working conditions are you looking for?
    b) Would you like the work itself?
    c) Will you earn enough money?
    d) Are the hours of work satisfactory?
    e) Do you have any physical problem you have to consider?
    f) Are you willing to travel on your job and/or work overtime?
    g) Are you willing to relocate?
    h) Will this job cause family problems?

5.   As you look at different occupations, think about:

- What each one involves (duties, responsibilities, working conditions and activities);
- What it requires from you (education, training, experience, personal qualifications); and
- What it has to offer you (opportunities for advancement, salary, benefits, skills).

Then relate the information to your list of what you want in an occupation. Keep narrowing your list until you're ready to make a choice. You could change jobs twenty times and work in five different occupations during your lifetime. Each decision you make will ultimately influence your career direction, *but you should be the one who chooses the path.*

6.   Start the decision-making process.

Next is the goal-setting stage in which you set concrete short-term and long-term goals to help you obtain your 'dream job.'

Sample short-term goal: to complete one course (name of course) towards obtaining a Business Administration Certificate, with a mark of over seventy percent before December 4th, 20 ___ .

Sample long-term goal: to complete all ten courses of a Business Administration Certificate with an average mark of over seventy percent before June 20___ .

All goals must specify requirements for quality, quantity and time (deadlines). You'll want to plan where and when you'll obtain the necessary training and/or education, what kind of company will provide the proper on-the-job training (if applicable), what knowledge you have to glean before being ready for the next step up and so on.

Goal-Setting Problems

Goal setting - intensive goal setting - is hard work. It takes a lot of effort and time. But *it's worth it.* If it takes you two years to decide where you want to go - that's okay, as long as you're steadily working towards finding the right occupation for you. Here are some goal setting problems that were related to me by participants of my Dynamic Goal Setting and Career Decisions seminars.

One woman had decided on an occupation, but found that other occupations started looking good and over-lapped her original goals. She kept thinking about all the other choices available to her. This happened because she hadn't fully investigated several options *before* making her decision.

When I started the process of choosing a career, the best prospect identified for me was sales. Selling was what I ended up doing (conducting training seminars where I sell ideas - one of the hardest things to sell). This is what counselling had pointed to all along. But I didn't start in sales; I wasn't ready at that time. It's also possible this woman, wasn't quite ready for the occupation she was best suited for. She might have to go around the periphery for a while until she gained confidence in her prime area of interest.

Then she would make sure her supervisor knew where she wanted to go and ask for his or her or help to get there, otherwise her supervisor might assume that she didn't have career aspirations at all. She could say: *'I'm really interested in a career in this department. Can you give me some idea of my chances for getting promoted and help me learn the things I need to be ready for that next step up?'* An empathetic boss would make sure she got the help she needed.

Mai Ling had worked for fourteen years with a company and had an outstanding reputation, but she was becoming bored and frustrated. She decided she had waited long enough, so she approached one of the vice-presidents and asked where the company was going in the next five years and how she could help it get there. She told him of her accomplishments and employment record.

Her timing couldn't have been better. He had been going over personnel files without much luck and she turned out to be the person he was looking for. He had never considered her for a promotion before (like most bosses he had just seen her as a woman - not as a potential executive). She was asked to head a new branch of the company. This would not have happened if she hadn't spoken to a person in authority.

A part-time employee wanted to know if she could talk to her employer the same way. Certainly she should! For example, she could say, *'I really enjoy working here. Do you think there's an opportunity for me to be taken on full-time? Here are the areas I'm interested in ... and my ultimate goal is ...'*

In short - ask for help - simply announce what you want. Your approach is as important as your request. If you're just saying, *'I need a better job, can you give me one?'* you're not likely to generate much interest. However, if you explain what *you* have to offer the company, you'll most likely get a hearing.

Another woman set a goal (to get an accounting degree) came close to achieving it and then found she was unhappy with her choice: *'I'm finding that accountants are kind of boring,'* she reported. *'I find I'm much more interested in management. Now I'm confused, because I've spent all those years towards something I don't want any more!'* I urged her to get career counselling to help her identify her transferrable skills. Her years of training could be of use in many other occupations than the one she chose initially.

Goal setting plan

When setting life or career goals for myself, I use the following plan to keep myself on track and make my goals more concrete and obtainable.

Step 1: Describe the situation as it is now.

Step 2: Describe the ideal situation.

Step 3: Identify the gap between 1 and 2 (your goal).

Step 4: List the driving and restraining forces.

Driving forces describe the benefits you'll derive when you reach your goal.

Restraining forces are the things that may be in your way and may keep you from reaching your goal.

Step 5: Brainstorm ways you will overcome restraining forces.

Step 6: Formulate plan of action.

- Steps or actions:
- Date or Time Limit:
- People to Involve:
- Resources Required:

Step 7: Implement your plan of action

Step 8: Evaluate the success of implementing your plan.

Goal setting will not get you that job, but putting your plan into action will. Don't allow yourself to get lazy; keep your momentum going by realising that you're constantly moving closer to your 'dream job.' Learn to be flexible. Bounce with the punches and keep your eyes open for unexpected opportunities to aid your career advancement.

Guidelines for setting career goals

1. Choose your career

85

The most important thing to remember when filling out tests and forms is that you can't 'fudge' the answers - they all have to be answered *as things are, not as you would like to pretend they are.* If you distort the truth of your situation, you won't come up with careers that suit your unique talents and abilities. You won't be able to accurately evaluate your strengths, weaknesses, likes and dislikes and to make a suitable career choice. After deciding on two or three occupations - determine if there is a market for that career. Choose your top career choice and then talk to at least two people in that profession. Ask them:

- What they like about their job;
- What they dislike about their job;
- What their average day entails;
- How did they get to the position they're in (what education and experience is necessary);
- If they had to do it all over again - would they still choose that profession?

2. Decide how you will get into your chosen occupation

When you've made a choice of career, use the ***Goal Setting Plan*** I've just identified, to decide how to get into the area you've chosen. This is where planning comes in. Don't procrastinate - do it now!

3. Find a position

This can be through word of mouth or through employment agencies, friends or by answering a newspaper or on-line advertisement. Employment agencies *don't* normally charge the applicant - they charge the employer - so apply with several - it won't cost you anything for their help.

If you're answering an advertisement, circle the verbs or action words used, then use those action words in your resume and covering letter. This will give you an edge over your competitors. Answer all questions asked in the advertisement, but be honest in your answers - don't lie. Recruiters look for similarities between your qualifications and job requirements.

4. Apply for the job

Many people don't like using resumes. Instead they rely on application forms and hope these will get them through the door for an interview. Unfortunately, this seldom works - so use a resume that 'sells' your unique talents and abilities. Usually, the only thing representing you prior to an interview is your resume. If it's inadequate, you simply won't be asked for an interview.

5. Attend an interview

If you're called for an interview, remember that you're there to sell yourself - don't let shyness keep you from 'tooting your own horn.' Know your strengths and weaknesses and be ready to discuss them with the interviewer. Have your facts clear in your mind, anticipate the interviewer's questions and have information handy that they may need. Make sure your physical appearance is neat and clean and that your apparel suits the position you're applying for. Do not wear jeans, shorts or sundresses to work or to an interview. Office workers are encouraged to wear apparel one step up from the position they're applying for.

How I obtained career counselling

When I re-entered the workforce (after spending fifteen years at home with my family) I was fortunate in meeting a highly skilled career counsellor. She became a friend and offered me her expertise. After I had completed all the necessary psychological, IQ and aptitude tests, she suggested five occupations, that with training, I could possibly excel at. None of the professions she suggested appealed to me.

You see, I had 'fudged' the test by answering the questions the way I *thought* she wanted me to, rather than analysing carefully what was the truth *for me*. For example, one question asked whether I'd rather be sitting at a typewriter typing (this was before computers) or fixing it with a screwdriver. The first time, I said I'd rather be typing (I typed about 85 wpm) when in reality I would much rather have been fixing it. I did the tests again *the right way* and thank goodness I did. It saved me many years of heartache that could have been spent in the wrong occupation. The five occupations that were suggested to me were:

1. **Selling goods or services**. Apparently, my persuasive powers were off the scale. At that particular time in my life, however, I

didn't believe I could sell my way out of a paper bag, so I said no to this choice.

2. **Marketing.** That sounded interesting to me. My counsellor advised me to speak to more than one person in each occupation I chose. This was to safeguard against getting negative information from people who may be in the wrong occupation themselves. (More than eighty percent of all people working are in the wrong job for them!) After interviewing several marketing specialists, I learned that there was far too much paperwork for my liking, so decided not to pursue marketing either.

3. **Public Relations.** After a bit of investigation, it appeared that this might be a suitable career for me. Then I learned there simply weren't enough jobs available to warrant taking the chance of being unemployed.

4. **Human Resources.** (At that time it was called Personnel). This involved a variety of tasks - recruitment of staff, employee relations, job descriptions, classification of jobs, wage and salary surveys, performance appraisals, exit interviews, training and development. I decided to investigate my fifth choice before making any firm decision.

5. **Small appliance repair person!** I knew I had an aptitude for mechanical and electrical things - but I'd never thought of it as a career for me. That was too far out for me to consider, as there were very few women in such 'non-traditional' jobs. (What amazes me is the fact that my second son chose large appliance repair as his occupation!)

After interviewing others, spending many hours of research and investigating occupations, I decided to pursue a career in human resources. I liked the variety it offered and the people contact. However, my counsellor wouldn't let me stop there. She explained that I needed to write down my goals to make sure that I remained focused. She taught me how to set long- and short-term goals. This was quite a chore because I'd never written goals for myself before.

Then she asked me to identify my specific goal relating to human resources. Did I wish to be a recruiter, to work in classification, look after company benefit plans? After much soul-searching, I decided to aim for a position as head of a human resources department. (At this time, there were very few women heads of *any* departments.)

My counsellor didn't laugh. Instead, she encouraged me to chart a path so I could reach my lofty objective. For instance: What education would I require and how and where would I obtain it? What kind of training and experience would I need to run a human resources department and where would I fill that need? Who would look after my children? How would I find the time to do all that I had to do?

My first sub-goal was to determine what education I'd need to get me where I wanted to go. With only a high-school diploma, I knew I'd have to obtain specific training. Instead of going to university full-time, I decided to obtain three evening certificate programs (which consisted of ten, thirty-nine-hour courses for each program). Within the next five years I obtained Business Administration, Marketing and Personnel Administration Certificates.

Then, I learned what kind of companies would provide the best environment for in-house training. A job with a small company probably wouldn't be very effective to meet my experience needs, because most wouldn't be able to spend the time to train me. I decided the best environment would be in a medium-to-large sized company, where I could learn the most up-to-date systems. I'd accept a position at a junior level and learn everything they could teach me about human resources - then go to on to another company and learn how they did everything. I found that there are many ways to perform personnel services - such as different methods of writing job descriptions, evaluating positions and conducting performance appraisals.

Before setting out on this venture, my career counsellor gave me invaluable advice by recommending that I set a backup goal as well. As she explained it, *'Let's say you've planned a trip to Hawaii; you took the trip and wondered why you felt so depressed when you got back. It's because you had no backup goal waiting on the back burner for you to start working on when you were close to achieving your first goal.'* She also advised me to specialise in more than one area (not putting all my eggs in one basket).

When asked what my backup goal would be, I decided it was to have my own company that would offer human resource management to

89

companies too small to have their own human resources departments. (I altered this later). As I came closer to achieving my first goal, I was encouraged to develop a specific plan for achieving the second one and to make sure that as I went along, everything I did in my private and business life was aimed towards achieving those goals.

Then I was urged to set time frames for achieving my goals. I decided it would take fifteen years to reach my first goal of becoming human resources manager. My second goal - having my own company - I estimated would take twenty years to reach.

A strange thing happened to these goals. Because I knew exactly where I wanted to go and how I intended to get there, I reached these goals long before I expected to! I had underestimated my abilities (as most women do). Within six years of setting my first goal (nine years ahead of schedule) I was appointed Human Resources Manager of not one, but a group of twelve construction companies. Eight years after setting my second goal (twelve years ahead of schedule) I opened my first training and development/management consulting firm in Edmonton, Alberta, Canada. Four years later, I opened the USA branch in Maui, Hawaii and in 1998 I emigrated to the Gold Coast of Queensland, Australia and opened a third branch.

Along the way, I set more goals so I could work in other occupations that used my transferrable skills. For over thirty years, my training and development firms offered over one hundred different training seminars in Australia, New Zealand, Canada, USA, Great Britain, Germany, South Africa, United Arab Emirates, Bahrain, Malaysia, Thailand, Hong Kong, Indonesia, Philippines and Singapore. I also marketed the sills of twelve associate trainers.

My company offers career counselling and provides human resources help to companies too small to have their own Human Resources Department. I've written twenty-three books (two of which have become international best-sellers). I've become a book publisher and have made my books available in paperback, eBook and Audio formats. I find my life very full and meaningful.

What are your career plans? Are you willing to spend the time and effort required to reach your goals? No one else can do this for you - so get busy and go for it!

Chapter Five

How to obtain the salary you're worth

Equal pay for work of equal value

> *'And the Lord spoke unto Moses, saying, 'Speak unto the children of Israel and say unto them: ... Thy valuation for the male from 20 years old even unto 60 years old, even thy valuation shall be 50 shekels of silver, after the shekel of the sanctuary. And if it be a female, then thy valuation shall be 30 shekels.'' (Leviticus, 27:1-4)*

Equal pay for work of equal value was obviously not practiced in Biblical times and has not been practiced since. Changing this value system is a slow and time-consuming process. Women have been fighting for wage parity for decades. Most people believe that the principle of equal pay for work of equal value means that a man and a woman doing essentially the same kind of work, should receive equal pay. But there's considerably more to it than that. Many laws already provide for equal pay for similar or substantially similar work in both the private and public sectors. Then, why do we still not have pay equity?

Job evaluation schemes rely on the judgement that certain skills and capacities are of greater value to an organisation and are therefore rewarded by status and higher pay. Many do not question the value of certain skills and the value of certain work. This omission is detrimental to women who traditionally have had their work and skills under-valued compared to those of most male workers.

These job evaluations rank jobs within the hierarchy of job worth, which is used for pay-setting purposes. Many organisations use qualitative methods to assess jobs against other jobs, either by comparing them to one another or by giving them a grade within a classification. They're broadly described in line with duties, responsibilities, basic knowledge and complexity of tasks, training, mental effort and skill requirements of the position.

Many employers have highly developed job-evaluation schemes that they insist provide equality for all. When formal job-classification systems were established decades ago, it was assumed that all work done by employees would be evaluated fairly. Salary ranges were chosen that were said to be fair for the duties performed. This scheme assigned points for factors such as knowledge, skill, effort and working conditions. Businesses were encouraged to implement fair classification systems for *all* positions, keeping in mind that *the position, not the person filling it,* was to be evaluated.

This method allowed companies to compare engineers with designers and secretaries with janitors. On the surface, this is what classification systems do. However, the criteria for assigning *merit* or importance to each kind of task is what's terribly out of whack. Lower salary ranges were usually assigned to traditionally female positions and discrimination was the result.

To this date, not much has changed. In many companies you'll find that only a small segment of employees (the middle group) has been evaluated fairly by their company's evaluation system. If lower and upper level positions are examined, it's often found that incorrect salary ranges have been allotted. In most cases, lower-level employees are underpaid - and upper-level staff is overpaid!

If these old job-classification systems had been implemented correctly, women working in personal assistant and clerical positions would have been paid as much as technicians, because of their specialised knowledge and skills. Many support positions require the same length of training and have similar working conditions as technologists' jobs. However, this is not reflected in the salary structures for the two types of jobs.

Worldwide, much effort has been put into dealing with gender bias in job evaluation systems. Many countries have found that legislative rulings were necessary to eliminate gender bias from the job evaluation process. Before this was implemented many women found:

- Gender-stereotyping which could result in the under-evaluation of female-held positions.

- Many evaluations of female-held positions underestimated the importance of the skills and qualities required.

Until recently, women accepted this type of inequity as their lot in life. But this is changing - it has to. As women understand business practices better, they learn that companies simply can't run without efficient support staff. However, many businesses believe that legislation to bring in equal pay for work of equal value - to equalise the salary structures for *different* but equally important jobs - will cripple their companies. In a way, you can't blame them for opposing such legislation. They believe they cannot afford to implement this policy in a tight economy and heaven forbid - they may have to take a pay cut themselves!

Business owners contend they can't afford to make these essential changes, but an imaginative approach to the problem would enable them to do so. Until pay equity is achieved, those who've been overpaid (according to fair and realistic job-evaluation criteria) would have their salaries frozen and those whose positions have been undervalued, would be paid a regular salary increase plus a portion of the increase that would normally have gone to the 'frozen' employee. Companies would not lose money under such a scheme, but we can see why there's such resistance to pay equity by the upper level decision-makers in industry. They're the ones who would be having their salaries frozen!

One example of pay inequity came to my attention when I was employed in a government Human Resources office in Canada. I conducted interviews to hire staff for its offices all over the province. At that time, there was an extremely high turnover of judicial clerks who worked in the court offices. When I looked at their job descriptions, I realised why this was occurring. Although they had the title 'clerk,' many were performing the duties of an office manager or department head.

The job description of a Judicial Clerk III read in part as follows: *'May act as Deputy Clerk or Deputy Sheriff; supervise, co-ordinate activities, direct preparation and maintenance of police court records; direct all seizure proceedings; direct sheriff's sale proceedings; direct and approve searches made in the Sheriff's office; act as Vital Statistics Registrar. Supervision received is very general in nature.'*

In many cases, these employees literally ran the court offices. Also, in many rural areas, when these clerks (mainly women) went on circuit with the judges, they were required not only to collect fines (which could be for considerable amounts of money - often in cash), but also to carry evidence for trials. This evidence could include such things as illegal drugs, alcohol or confiscated weapons. These clerks often travelled alone to the different judicial offices and had no weapons with which to protect themselves. A judicial enquiry into this situation was begun and the necessary adjustments were (finally) implemented after completion of the Kirby Report *twelve years later*! In the meantime, the high turnover of judicial clerks continued to the detriment of everyone involved with the court system in that province.

Part-time workers

Part-time workers (almost three-quarters of whom are women) are also fighting for fair wages and benefits. In every occupational category, part-time workers receive lower pay than full-time workers. This is one of the main reasons why eighty percent of unemployed women want full-time, rather than part-time work. Full-time employees' company benefits often add thirty percent or more to their salary. Part-time workers believe that these benefits should be pro-rated, based on the number of hours they work. At present, part-time employees receive at best six percent vacation and statutory holiday pay. However, many of these 'part-time' workers put in as much as forty hours a week, with *no* company benefits! Their employers are getting a free ride at their employees' expense.

A variety of excuses are given for paying women less than men. It may be assumed that a married woman doesn't need a high salary, but a man has 'a family to support' so should be paid more. The assumption is often made that a divorced woman is receiving huge alimony or child-support payments or that a single woman's 'dates' pay for all her entertainment. But whether or not a woman has a man to lean on financially (and many do *not*) is completely beside the point. The state of the employee's personal life has nothing to do with what s/he should be paid for doing a specific job. The job is given the value, not the person filling it.

If your employer throws these outdated excuses at you - defend yourself. Women pay rent, utilities, income tax and so on - just as men do - and they have a right to expect comparable salaries. Discrimination in wages still persists and women must fight if they wish to escape from the pink-collar ghetto. As it stands now, women are subsidising businesses and this has to stop!

94

When job evaluations are completed properly, the next step for a woman wanting to get ahead in business is to be able to sell her skills and abilities to a potential employer.

Selling yourself in an interview

Two equally talented women applied for a job. The first woman explained that she was a single mom who really needed the job. She explained that she was a hard worker and would take any job the company felt she could handle.

The second woman spent most of her part of the interview speaking about the skills and abilities she was offering to the company.

Which woman would you hire? The one who was asking the employer *'What can you do for me?'* or the one who told the employer, *'These are the skills and abilities I bring to your company. Do you have a position that will use those skills?'* For obvious reasons, the employer chose the second applicant.

On an interview, be sure to explain what *you* can do for a company (not what *they* can do for you)! Define your unique qualities. For instance, if you were applying for a supervisory position, you'd give all the qualities you possess that make you a good supervisor. Here are a few more tips to remember when applying for a position:

1. Learn whether you should use a **Chronological** resume (experience listed in date order starting with the most recent position). This is normally used if you are staying within your own occupation;

   Or a **Functional** resume (listing your transferrable skills). This is often used if you are applying for positions that are not within your normal occupation or where you want to identify your transferrable skills.

   Combination Resume: As you'd expect - it's a combination of the Chronological and Functional Resumes. Not only does it identify the person's transferrable skills, but also identifies the companies where those skills were gained. Instead of elaborate information about what the person did for the companies, just the company, position and dates of employment are identified after your transferrable skills are given.

95

Or, a **Portfolio** (showing examples of your work). This could be used by engineers, draftspersons, models etc. in addition to a chronological or functional resume.

I use a chronological resume when a company asks me to do human resources work for them. If I'm asked to conduct training seminars, I use a functional resume. On a first interview with a potential client for training, I also take my portfolio with sample brochures prepared by the hundreds of companies world-wide who have offered my seminars and letters of reference from satisfied international clients.

2. Before the interview, research to obtain as much information as possible about the vacant position. Go on-line or ask at your local library. Check directories and examine the company's annual report. Learn how large the company is, what products it manufactures or what services it provides. Check with your local newspapers to see if they have a clipping file about the company. You'll be able to learn about current and future projects the company is pursuing. Have a written list of questions related to this research, to ask during the interview.

Interview tips

1. Be on time for the interview - in fact be early, so you can check your appearance and review your information regarding the company and the position.
2. Let *them* interview *you*. You'll usually have time near the end of the interview to ask questions. Make sure you have several job-related questions ready. Don't concentrate on salary and benefits.
3. Don't be put off by panel interviews (more than one person). There are advantages to panel interviews.

    o Normally there's a representative from the Human Resources Department. This person explains company benefits, pension plan, etc., knows how to keep others at the interview on track and will stop illegal questions from being asked by others on the panel.

    o There's less potential for bias or prejudice.

o The supervisor (if present) usually has more specific information about the job itself (your co-workers, the number of staff in the area, the nature of the job itself).

o The third person may be the supervisor's supervisor or possibly another supervisor (if there's more than one vacancy).

4. When you arrive for the interview ask the receptionist for the name(s) of the interviewer(s). In your mind, repeat the name(s) until you know them by heart. When you're taken into the interview room, *you* should offer your hand for a handshake. Make sure you know how to shake hands properly. No wishy-washy handshakes. If you have problems in this area, practice until you're comfortable.

5. At the interview, don't be afraid to *'toot your own horn'* and sell your talents and abilities. No one else is likely to do it for you. But don't lie! Talk loudly enough for them to hear you easily, but if you're nervous, watch that the pitch of your voice doesn't rise.

6. Give concise, clear answers and try to avoid rambling. Keep all answers job-related. If you happen to forget the question, don't be ashamed to say so; they know you're nervous and won't be turned off by this.

7. Never bad-mouth a former employer or company. This only makes *you* look bad and it just isn't done by successful people.

8. Know how to deal with illegal interview questions. To learn about illegal interview questions, contact your Human Rights and Equal Opportunity Commission and find out what these questions are. For example, questions relating to the private life of the person aren't allowed, either on the application form or during the interview.

Discrimination and Human Rights

Here are some sample interview questions that cannot be asked in Alberta, Canada (these will not likely be the same in your area - so it's up to you to check your local laws):

1. What Church do you attend? (They're allowed to ask what you do with your spare time or what business-related organisations you belong to).

2. Are you married? What does your spouse do? Where does he work? Inquiries into family circumstances, relationships, spouses' situation, family planning or any related circumstances are not acceptable. Applicant may be asked if she is willing and able to be transferred, to travel, to work weekends or shifts or overtime and under what conditions.

3. How many children do you have? How old are they? What are their names and ages? How are they cared for?

4. What would your spouse think of your working overtime? Would you have to pick up your children at a certain time?

5. What would your spouse think of your having to travel with your job or stay overnight in some other city?

6. How old are you? What's your birth date? (They're able to ask questions if they relate to age restrictions because of licensing only).

7. I see you're married - what are your plans for having a family? Are you pregnant? When was your last period? (Yes, this question has been asked!)

8. This job is usually a field that is male dominated. What problems do you foresee if we offered this position to you?

9. Have you had any sexual harassment at any of your past employers?

10. I see you've had to leave your past two positions because your spouse was transferred. Do you anticipate this will happen again in the near future?

11. Where were you born? Where are your ancestors from? What is your national or ethnic origin? No inquiries indicating national or ethnic origin may be made except those relating to entitlement to work. This includes references to birthplace, mother tongue, nationality or foreign residence. Questions relating to a person's race, colour, complexion, hair or skin colour should not be asked. No information should be asked about relatives - including names, addresses and relationships to the applicant. The names(s) and addresses of person(s) to be notified in the case of an emergency may be required *after* the selection decision has been made.

12. Any physical disabilities? (Can only be asked if duties require heavy lifting or other physical job requirements.)

13. Physical characteristics. (Only one allowed - job offer is dependent on passing a job-related physical or medical examination).
14. Photographs may not be requested prior to the interview. Photographs may be required for identification purposes *after* appointment.

Application Forms

(These are illegal questions or requests. Again make sure you check the laws in your area.)

1. Mr. Mrs. Miss Ms or male, female;
2. Height, weight, hair and eye colour;
3. Please submit a recent photograph;
4. Race or colour;
5. Religious affiliation;
6. Birthplace, place of origin, ancestry or citizenship, status of parents, grandparents. (Can ask - are you legally permitted to work in this country?)
7. Christian name, maiden name. (Can ask: name used in previous employment and/or education, for purposes of reference checks.)
8. Languages (Can ask if fluency in a language is a requirement of the job).
9. Date of Birth (Can ask: Have you reached age of majority or questions relating to licensing regulations).

What can and cannot be asked on application forms and at interviews?

Requesting unnecessary information that may be used later to discriminate - is against the law. The key is that only questions that are directly relevant to the job should be asked. It's inappropriate to ask questions (either on application forms or during the interview) about the following:

• Marital status;
• Sex and age;
• Number of children:

- Spouse's name;
- Country of birth:
- General health;
- Sick leave record;
- Religion;
- Criminal record: (unless it is a job requirement)
- Blue card (unless it is a job requirement for working with children, the elderly or disabled)
- Sexual preference;
- Political affiliation;
- Union membership;
- Height and weight;
- Occupation of spouse:
- Workers' compensation record.

Employment application forms should only seek information needed by organisations to assess the qualifications and skills of applicants to perform the work for which they hold themselves capable. Irrelevant and unnecessary questions may give the appearance of discrimination. The language used on the application form should be non-sexist and the same core questions should be asked of female and male applicants on application forms and on the interview.

For example: If the job involves travel and/or regular overtime, *all* applicants must be asked whether they're able to do these things - rather than only female applicants being asked whether they have made arrangements for childcare and housework. Employers are advised to stay clear of what might be considered illegal questions such as:

- Who will look after your children while you work?
- Who picks them up after school?
- Are you married?
- Are you planning a family?
- What country did you come from?
- When did you come to this country?
- Does your spouse work?
- What if your husband got a transfer?
- How old are you?

100

Questions women are often asked on interviews

Many women are still asked questions that are clearly illegal and find themselves in a quandary on how to reply to them. To make it easier for you to deal with these questions, estimate why the interviewer is asking the questions and what s/he really wants to know. Let's look at two of the illegal questions that are often asked of women: *'Are you married? Are you thinking of starting a family soon?'* Most women would just like to reply, *'Don't you realise that your questions are illegal?'*

You can imagine how potential employers would react! It would be better if you asked yourself what do they *really want to know*? What's behind these questions is the unasked one, *'What are your career plans for the next five years?'* (They're afraid you won't stay long enough in the position). When you've made this mental translation, your answer could be: *'I assume you want to know my career plans. I intend to devote the next ten years of my life to my career.'*

If they ask, *'Do you have any children,'* what they're likely wanting to know is your attendance record. If they ask, *'Would your husband object if we later needed to transfer you to another city?'* Their question should have been, *'Would you be willing to re-locate if we needed to transfer you to another city?'* Or, if they ask, *'Who picks your children up at day care?'* what they should have asked is, *'Can you work overtime when required?'* After you've identified what they *really* want to know, answer the perceived question.

Do this with all the illegal questions that are thrown your way. It still won't prevent potential employers from asking them, but at least you'll be able to live with the answers you give. Many women come away from this kind of interview feeling soiled because they've answered these illegal questions and felt terrible that they allowed themselves to be subjected to harassment by a potential employer. With such high unemployment, many are reluctant to antagonise a possible employer. However, if you feel the need to object more strongly, you can lodge a complaint with your local Human Rights or Equal Opportunity commission because they *did* ask illegal questions on the interview. Make sure you clearly document the questions asked at these interviews for future reference.

Employers should remember that if the question does not apply to your qualifications to do the job – the question should not be asked.

Tricky interview questions

Interviewers may also ask such tricky questions as:

- Why do you think you would like to work for this company?
- Why should I hire *you* for this position?
- What are your strengths/weaknesses?
- Tell me about yourself.

Employment interview questions

Here are some common interview questions. Anticipate that you'll be asked several of them. Prepare, by rehearsing your answers to the following questions:

1. What are your future career plans? (You had better have a two- or five-year career plan ready to explain.)
2. What is your ultimate career goal? What steps have you taken to achieve this goal?
3. What positions have you held? How were they obtained and why did you leave?
4. How do you spend your spare time?
5. What are your hobbies? (They want to know if you have a variety of interests, which would likely make you more flexible on the job.)
6. What kind of position interests you most?
7. What do you know about our company? (Prepare carefully for this one. I'll explain how to do this later.)
8. What qualifications do you have that make you believe you'll do well in this position?
9. Do you prefer to work in any specific geographic location? Why?
10. What personal characteristics are necessary for success in your chosen field? Do you feel you have those characteristics?
11. Why do you think you'd like this particular type of position?
12. Do you prefer working with others or by yourself?
13. What kind of supervision do you prefer? (Close supervision - so you're absolutely sure you know what your supervisor wants

from you? Or do you prefer a more loose supervision, where your employer gives you a task and you decide how to complete it?)

14. How did your previous employers treat you? (Be careful not to bad-mouth or show other signs of discord if possible).

15. What interests you about our product (or service)?

16. Do you like routine work?

17. What kind of people would you rather not work with?

18. Do you enjoy sports as a participant or as an observer?

19. Have you worked as part of a team before? At work? In sports?

20. What jobs have you enjoyed the most? The least? Why?

21. What are your own special abilities? (Toot your own horn here!)

22. Do you prefer a large or small department to work in? Why?

23. Do you like to travel on the job? How much?

24. Would working overtime be a problem?

25. Have you ever supervised others before? Under what circumstances? How large a staff? Have you received any supervisory training?

26. Have you ever been fired from a position in the past? Why?

27. Were you ever asked to resign?

28. What kind of energy level do you feel you have?

29. Are you a high, medium or low achiever?

30. Is your energy level higher in the morning, afternoon or evening? (This could be relevant if your company offers shift work.)

31. What causes you stress in a work environment?

32. How do you relieve stress when it becomes a problem?

33. How was your attendance at your last position? What were the main reasons for absenteeism? (They'll want to know whether your absences relate to sick family members or if you have chronic illnesses of your own).

34. What kind of training do you feel you'd need if we offered you the position?

35. What are your salary expectations? (Prepare for this by making enquiries about the salary range of the position *before* the interview and be ready to negotiate for a higher salary). See topic at the end of this chapter entitled: *'How to Obtain the Salary You're Worth.'*

36. When are you available for employment? (Don't give too soon a date because you'll want a written job offer before you give notice to your present employer.)
37. If I were to contact your former employer, what kind of reference do you think they'd give me? (You might take along a copy of your latest performance appraisal. If you don't have one, be sure to talk to your past and/or present supervisors to see what kind of reference they'd give you).
38. Tell me about yourself. (If you answer this question by telling them your life story, you'll miss out on an ideal opportunity to sell yourself.)
39. What are your major strengths? (Again this is an opportunity to 'toot your own horn.')
40. What are your major weaknesses? (Be prepared for this one otherwise you're likely to become flustered.) Try to keep things positive. For example: *'I try to do too many things at one time. I've just taken a time management course and have learned how to prepare `to do' lists and set priorities. I don't think I'll have problems in this area in the future.'*
41. Why should we hire you? (I always encourage employers to ask this one! Be ready to sell your skills and abilities).

Prepare before an interview and decide how to reply to these questions. Know the reasons why you would like to work for the company. Explain why you feel you're well qualified for the position.

The question *'What are your strengths?'* often causes candidates to dry up - so be prepared for it. Have at least three or four things you feel you can do better than most people. Try it now. Write down what you think your strengths are. If you're having problems doing so, ask a friend or family member to help you. For example:

'I'm extremely good at organising things (give examples of complex things you've organised).'
'I have very good interpersonal skills (give examples).'
'I have the ability to motivate people beyond their normal level of production.'
'I'm a high achiever and have high expectations for myself and my staff. (But be aware that the latter could be seen as a weakness - expecting too much of your staff.)'

'I'm a self-starter and I work well without supervision.'

These are the kinds of things employers want to hear. They don't care that you're a good swimmer or good at sports or a good mother. It's job-related strengths they want to learn about.

Be willing to discuss your weaknesses too. Can you identify your weaknesses? Take time to write these down right now. Many women have a tough time with this one, especially those who've never applied for a senior position. Often you can use your weaknesses to your advantage. For instance, when you investigated the position, you may have found that the company wanted someone who worked well without supervision and who could handle crisis situations on their own.

You could explain that one of your weaknesses is that you have problems dealing with red tape. What does that tell your potential employer? That you're capable of making many very quick decisions, based on the information at hand. In essence, what you do is turn around what could be considered a negative trait and make it sound positive.

Another approach that often works is to explain that you're not very well organised but you're correcting the problem by attending time-management classes, using day timers and 'to do' lists. As well, outline other things you're doing to be better organised in the future. Whatever your failings are, describe what you're doing to correct them or don't mention them at all!

'Tell me about yourself.' How are you likely to answer this question? As with the *'strengths/ weaknesses'* questions, use this chance to identify your good points. Don't miss this opportunity to sell yourself!

Interviews for senior positions differ from those of clerical or support-staff positions. In senior positions, you'll most likely work under pressure, interview others and have to be a good decision-maker, so they're likely to throw much more complex questions at you. There will probably be more than one person interviewing you and it may seem like more of a grilling session - with you in the hot seat. Be ready for this experience. Just know your facts and don't let them rattle you. If you do find yourself getting rattled, take a deep breath and make a conscious effort to answer their questions calmly and clearly. Slow down your speech and control the level of your voice.

If they ask you a question you can't answer, admit it. If they throw one at you about a situation you've never encountered, say, *'I've never been in that situation before. Give me a minute to think this one over ... I would ...'* Let your intuition give you your best answer.

What do you do if they won't let you finish your statement, but go on to the next question before you're finished? Say, *'Before I answer this question, I'd like to finish answering the last one.'* Answer the first question and then handle the second one. By this time you may have forgotten the second question and you may have to ask them to repeat it. By following this strategy, you make them give you an opportunity to answer *all* their questions. You're taking control of the situation and they'll realise that they can't put you off balance.

How to obtain the salary you're worth

Women who want equal pay for work of equal value need to stand up for themselves and negotiate for the salaries they're worth - just as successful men do. Look at the full package deal - not just the salary. This includes extended holidays, a larger office and support staff. Make sure the company pension plan benefits are the same for women as for men.

Companies normally offer a woman a lower salary than a man, so before you go to an interview, do your homework by determining the salary range of the position you're applying for. Obtain this information by calling the company representative who's responsible for filling the vacancy. Some may be reluctant to give you the salary range. If they balk, say, *'I need to know the salary range because I'm afraid I might be overqualified for the position.'* They'll usually give the salary range to you.

Let's suppose you haven't learned the salary range before an interview and the recruiter asks, *'What are your salary expectations?'* We'll say you're earning an annual salary of $32,000 in your present position, but you know there are more responsibilities in the new position. You say that your salary expectations are $35,000 and feel you'll be happy with a $3,000 a year raise.

Not a wise move! If you'd done your homework, you might have found that the salary range for this position (normally filled by a male) was $40,000 to $45,000. You goofed! Of course they're going to hire you for $35,000! But you'll be grossly underpaid for what you'll be doing - from the start of your employment and thereafter.

Now let's assume you've done your homework and learned that the salary range was $40,000 to $45,000. What should you answer when asked, *'What are your salary expectations?'* Would you say $40,000 (as most women would) or $44,000 (as most men would)? So your reply should be the same, *'$44,000.'* They're bound to negotiate with you and you'll probably end up settling for about $42,500 for your starting salary. That's $7,500 per year more than the $35,000 you were originally willing to take! Quite a difference!

Unfortunately, your original bad choice doesn't end there. The woman who accepted the $35,000 starting salary would probably qualify for a cost-of-living increase after a year with the company. Let's say it's three percent. This would bring her salary up to $36,750. The second year's increase is the same, so her salary would go up to $38,587. If however, she had obtained the $42,500 salary - after a year she'd be making $44,625 and after two years - $46.956. This would be $8,267 more! The gap is increasing between what she should have been paid and what she agreed to accept and the gap will get larger as time goes on.

If the recruiter asks what she was earning in her last position, she would be wise to explain that she was in a much more junior position, so her present salary isn't relevant to the position she's applying for (unless it's close to the salary range they're offering).

Initially, you may find it difficult negotiating this way, but you must feel you're worth it. Remember, *employers wouldn't assign salary ranges to these positions, if they weren't worth the dollar amount.*

Written job offers

After you've given a verbal *'Yes'* to a job offer, ask when you can expect to receive their written job offer.

Under no conditions, should you accept an oral job offer and give notice to your present employer - without first receiving a written job offer from the new company.

Why is this important? The new company can back out, leaving you with no job at all. A written job offer is equivalent to a contract in a court of law. Most companies mail or e-mail confirmation letters to their new employees spelling out the salary and benefits they've agreed on. This letter should confirm:

1. Salary agreed upon when the oral offer was accepted;
2. Title of the position you will hold;
3. Starting date and hours of employment;
4. Name and title of the person you report to and where and when you report;
5. Type and amount of relocation assistance (if required);
6. Length of the probationary period; if any.

It may also spell out the date of your first salary increase. Make sure the letter states the length of your probationary period. If it's one year, that's a long time and you'll be in an uncertain position until it's over. An employer can terminate an unacceptable employee at any time during this probationary period without going through formal disciplinary procedures (although the employer still has to document why the employee was unsuitable). As well, most company benefits may not be given to new employees until their probationary period is over.

If at all possible, try to get a three-month probationary period with a promise of a salary review after that time. After all, you won't be the novice you were when the company hired you three months earlier. You'll have learned the duties of the position and be more efficient in handling your duties - therefore you'll deserve more pay.

Less work - more pay

Employees who are paid by the hour (except those in the trades) receive the lowest salaries; employees paid by the week are next. Supervisors' salaries are usually quoted in annual terms. Knowing this, you can judge from an advertisement where you would fit into the corporate structure when it comes to discussing salary at the end of an interview. Note, too, that if your future boss doesn't interview you for your new job - the job probably isn't important. If routine, repetitive work takes up eighty to ninety percent of your job - it's probably a dead-end position with little chance for promotion.

Asking for a raise

Can you remember a time in your past when you asked for a raise? Many women have *never* asked for a raise. They assume that if they do they're being 'pushy.' They believe management sees this as a negative trait. If you did ask for a raise, were you successful? I'll bet most of you were - simply because you had the initiative to ask. Men do it automatically. Women often think the company will *'get mad at them'* and they might get fired. This isn't what happens. The worst that will happen is that you'll be told, *'No.'* If a man can say, *'It's been fifteen months and I haven't received a raise. It's time don't you think?'* so can you.

This is the sort of thing you should try to find out when you're hired; it shouldn't have to be guesswork after you've taken the job. When you receive your verbal job offer, ask what kind of salary increases you can expect and if the company has salary reviews on a regular basis. Determine if the company has regular performance appraisals and if so, how often they're done. Ask whether merit (or cost-of-living) increases coincide with the performance appraisal.

Do they have merit increases as well as cost-of-living increases? Don't always assume that if your company gives a three percent cost-of-living increase that you're going to get three per cent. One employee might get one percent and another five percent, depending on individual performance. These raises are often tied into a merit system. So if you get a one percent raise, what they're telling you is that you weren't giving them even average performance - that your work is determined to be below average. If you feel this isn't true, fight their decision with facts. Tell them why you think you were at least average or possibly higher. (Unionised workers or those working in award positions are an exception to these rules; their raises are more structured.)

Let's say it's getting close to the end of your probation period (June 1st). Don't wait until June 1st to do something. Instead, on May 15th remind your boss that your probationary period will be up on June 1st. Then on May 31st, ask your boss what time s/he can see you on June 1st to discuss your salary increase. Some bosses still believe that if you don't ask for a raise - that money isn't important to you.

In your negotiations, avoid issuing the ultimatum that you'll quit if you don't get a raise. They just might take you up on it! Instead, document extra projects you've been doing since your last raise and bring these to your boss's attention. Prove you're worthy of a raise! If they don't give you one, you deserve to know why.

If you're working for a boss who's recently received a substantial promotion, make sure you ask for a raise too, especially if you're in a support position. If your boss gets a raise - so should you - because guess who helped him or her get there? Also, if your boss has taken on more responsibility, your job classification will likely change because your responsibilities and consequence of error ratio will also be greater.

Unfortunately some bosses don't take you along with them when they receive a promotion. You might have to remind your boss that you were part of his or her success and that you're ready for the new support position that goes along with his or her promotion. Try it - you have nothing to lose.

Have you ever been overlooked for a promotion? Learn how to deal with that situation in Chapter 6.

Chapter Six

How to handle being overlooked for a promotion and other work-related problems

The most important thing to remember when involving yourself in any kind of negotiation or confrontation with management is to keep your 'cool!' Many women cry when they become angry. Do everything you can to avoid this by rehearsing the situation until it's no longer an emotional issue with you. Rehearse what you're going to say with a close friend. Try to ensure that your friend is a good negotiator who can play 'the boss' well. This person should confront you with difficult things that are relevant to the situation you're going to face and every roadblock the boss is likely to throw at you.

Practice until you can respond - not with anger or tears - but as if you're acting a part. Learn to pull yourself mentally away from the situation by pretending you're negotiating on behalf of another person. You'll become less emotionally involved. Use a tape recorder to rehearse what you're going to say until it becomes automatic.

Learn not to raise the pitch or your voice, which women tend to do when they're angry or stressed. This tells your employer that you've lost control of your side of the negotiations and helps him or her keep the upper hand. Remain calm while you state your case (which you have supported with facts). You may find that this was all that was necessary - to state your case using facts, not emotions.

Have you ever been overlooked for a promotion or possibly you didn't even know the job was available and someone else was hired? Did the idea of facing the decision-makers make you hesitate to speak to them? Unless you confront this inequity, it simply won't change. Here are some steps you can take to stop this from happening in the future:

Consider this situation. There's a promotional position in your company that you've applied for because you believe you're well qualified for it. You submit your resume for consideration and learn that someone else has been hired for the position. You *know* this person is less qualified than you so you're rightfully upset. Is it too late to do something about it? No, it isn't. What steps should you take? How should you approach this situation? Simply complaining to the hiring supervisor or saying, *'How come you hired somebody who's less qualified than I?'* will not likely work.

Instead, contact the supervisor who was in charge of hiring for the position and ask for fifteen minutes of his time (we'll assume that it's a man). If he asks why, explain that it's important for you to obtain some information regarding the position. He'll have his guard up, but if you're persistent he'll see you. He expects you to attack him and will be on the defensive, even before you enter the room, so your approach has to be non-threatening. (The hard-nosed approach of most labour negotiations won't work in this situation.)

You may object to this softer approach and feel that pussyfooting around someone who has been unfair is impossible. However, in my experience, this approach works much better than a direct angry confrontation. You accomplish the same end, but nobody gets defensive.

Start by being honest and admit that you're upset. Say, *'You know that I was really looking forward to being accepted for this position and I'm upset that I wasn't chosen. Can you help me determine what I'm missing in my background that's keeping me from being promoted?'* He'll feel he's somewhat off the hook because you're discussing your failings, not questioning the decision. If he says, *'The other person was just better qualified than you,'* your response should be, *'Could you be more specific about the qualifications that are necessary for the job?'* After he's pointed out the qualifications, paraphrase what he's said and add, *'I have that kind of experience - in fact, I have more than you've said is necessary for that position, so I guess that isn't the problem.'*

He'll have to admit you're right. *'No, I guess not. You have seven years' experience in that area.'* (You know that George, who got the job, has only five years' experience. Don't throw this at the supervisor - store this information for later.)

Next ask, *'What other kinds of qualifications were necessary for this position?'* He may suggest some additional type of knowledge or experience and your reply might be: *'I don't think that's a problem either.'* Here you would give further facts showing that you have those qualifications as well (assuming you do). In short, keep giving

112

factual reasons why you don't think his explanation eliminates you as a candidate. He'll try to pull out some plausible reason why you didn't get the job and he won't be able to do it.

At the end of the interview, say something like, *'Well, I don't know where this leaves us, because it appears that, from what you've just told me, I was the best qualified for the job. As you stated, as far as experience is concerned, I needed five years' experience and I have seven. I know George only has five. As far as education goes, I have ... and I know George has only ... I'm still at a loss to know why he got the job and I didn't. What do we do now?'*

You've put this person on the spot. You've presented your facts in such a way where it can't be denied that you're right. Many would say that all you've done is make the person angry. This may be so, but the supervisor will be angry because you're right and he's wrong. This may be the time to ask for an impartial person to be involved. If you're in a union environment, your steward could be called in to mediate. If it's a non-union environment, a representative of the Human Resources Department could be called in to solve the dilemma.

Another choice could be to mark time and leave the meeting with this comment; *'Well, it's unfortunate that this happened. I really feel upset, because we both know that I should have been given the job. Can I count on you to see that I won't be overlooked for the next promotion?'*

This type of approach is low-key without being wishy-washy. You keep your cool - and your temper - but also give yourself a better chance of being treated fairly in the future. It might put the company in a very difficult position if you demand that they pull back the promotion they've already offered to George. If George had been given a written job offer, he would be able to sue the company. You may have let the company off the hook. They may even recommend you for a promotion in another department. In fact, that's one of the things you can ask them to do.

Would you feel comfortable doing it this way? I hope so. It's a win/win situation. However, you might conclude that this approach isn't for you, depending on how strongly you feel about the situation. You may say to yourself, *'I don't give a hoot about this company. I'm going to fight this; a principle is at stake here. I'm not going to sit idly by and let someone else take the position that should have been mine!'* and take the issue to the top. Your first step would be to speak to your Human Resources Manager. If your company's too small to have one, speak to a senior official. If s/he doesn't help, lodge a complaint with the Human Rights and Equal Opportunities Commission.

Acting positions

An acting position occurs when your boss goes away and puts you in charge of his or her job. There should be some monetary compensation, because you'll be handling your job and theirs at the same time. Before accepting this kind of assignment, ask if you'll be paid more for those duties. It's better to know, before making your decision. If they say no - ask why. You might decide that you want and need this kind of experience because it will look good on your resume. Being able to say that you've worked as an acting supervisor might be something you want. Judge for yourself whether you'll insist on being paid more.

Many people assume that because they've filled an acting position, they're automatically going to be promoted into that position when it becomes available. Not so. Companies may even hire someone off the street. You may feel like asking the person in charge why you're good enough to work in an acting capacity, but not good enough to handle the job now that it's open. Before complaining, check the prerequisites of the job. Is it possible that you're missing important education or training? If so, ask your boss to help you obtain this training. If you *are* qualified - back up your statements with facts about why you should have received the promotion.

Guard against being overlooked for promotions in future by making sure your boss knows your career plans or talk to people in your Human Resources department. Ask them to watch for any promotional opportunities that might help you get where you want to go. Otherwise, no matter how good your qualifications are - you might be overlooked again. The oversight may be unintentional - the result of conditioning.

It's also a good idea to ask your supervisor what s/he feels is missing in your training or background that might be keeping you from being promoted. A boss who is on your side can be a great ally because

114

s/he will be spending time and effort towards helping you get where you want to be. Ask your supervisor to help you obtain the necessary training or experience and to recommend you for the promotions s/he thinks fit your qualifications.

OTHER WORK PROBLEMS

The 'Leap-frog' Syndrome

Have you ever trained someone and then watched that person get the promotion instead of you? Follow the same advice I gave earlier in this chapter and approach your boss about it. If your employer favours your male co-workers for training or promotional opportunities and you've been turned down, complain to the Human Rights and Equal Opportunities Commission. But if you can't prove sex-based discrimination or you prefer not to complain formally, there are several more informal but effective options you can try.

Organise a status-of-women committee with your female co-workers to approach your employer with positive suggestions for the training, development and promotion of women.

Let your Human Resources Department know about your interest in existing employee training programs and/or suggest new ones to them.

Check out local adult-education courses to expand your own horizons. (You may have to pay for this yourself.)

The Dead-end Job

At one of my seminars a participant asked: *'How do I handle a situation where I started a job in a department where there was plenty to learn (that's why I took the job) but no one will allow me to learn more? My job duties are done long before the day is over, so I've asked for more responsibility and have even asked co-workers for some of their work. My boss has objected and my co-workers are a little cool with me.'*

If she is given a higher level of responsibility in her position, she'll also be placed in a higher job classification, which will put her into a higher pay range. Her boss knows this will happen. And if she attempts to do some of the tasks of her co-workers, they might

115

assume that she's trying to take over their jobs. This could be very threatening to them. It sounds as if she was hired into a position for which she was overqualified in the first place and the position offered little room for growth and development of her abilities. Her best course of action would be to apply for more senior positions.

Foot-dragging co-workers

Another participant Margaret said her co-workers didn't seem to know how to deal with deadlines; they extended them all the time. She explained that when they were wasting time she got mad and would tell them to work harder. I asked her if she supervised them and she admitted they were co-workers rather than her subordinates. I explained to her that she was acting out the role of a supervisor (without the authority) by criticising her co-workers' work. Naturally they objected and were probably thinking, *'Who does she think she is?'*

She was responsible for only her own work - not that of her co-workers. The person responsible for the performance of her co-workers was the supervisor. Her best course of action would be to back off and make sure she does her own work properly.

Another participant, Della, inquired, *'I feel I'm doing far more work than my two co-workers, who waste a lot of time taking personal calls and talking to each other.'* The supervisor's help is needed here. First of all, Della would gather details and be sure of her facts. For instance, let's say there's a pool of work that she and two other employees do as time permits. She should try to determine some measuring tool that would show how much each employee accomplishes. For example; this could be done by counting the number of files processed each day and who handled each file. She might find that thirty files are processed in a normal day.

It wouldn't take long for the supervisor to recognise that the two lazy co-workers are averaging eight or nine files each a day and Della is averaging twelve to fourteen. The supervisor must then determine whether the work is being done accurately. If all accuracy rates are the same - there's no problem for Della. But if the one doing the most files (Della) is making more mistakes, she should be encouraged to slow down and do fewer files.

116

Let's assume, though, that the accuracy rate was the same for all three workers. The supervisor could call the three workers into her office. She would give them the information she's gathered regarding the number of files completed in the department and explain that in future, each employee would be delegated ten files each per day to process. Problem solved. Della does not need to accuse the two slower workers of not doing their share. With her supervisor's help, they now know what's expected of them. This, of course, takes a supervisor who is fair and just. Analyse your supervisor - would s/he go along with this tactic?

Dumping or 'Job Enlargement'

Marcie figured that most of her duties fell under the catch-all phrase *'Other duties as assigned.'* If more than ten percent of your duties fit into this category, your job description is inaccurate. If your company is using an official job-classification system, they know this is the percentage allowed. Have your job description re-written with realistic information about the tasks you perform (including weekly, monthly or yearly assignments).

Marcie's next problem was how to reply when her supervisor started every new task with the statement: *'It's a marvellous opportunity. How can you refuse an opportunity that might get you ahead?'* If these opportunities will really teach her something she wouldn't learn any other way and that she needs for her next step up – she should grab them. Keep in mind that her boss is actually teaching her how to do his or her job. As far as development goes, it's to her advantage to accept. When she's interviewed for her next promotion, she'll be able to say: *'I was given this project to do by my boss and I handled it well.'* She'll be able to prove she's capable of doing the duties of the more demanding position.

But what if that *'opportunity'* is really just an addition to her workload and makes it harder for her to stay on top of her work? If her company is really dumping on her, then we're getting into what's called *'job enlargement.'* This term means that they're giving her more of the same level of tasks. This often happens when companies cut staff. Four people are often doing the work that five used to do. Effective time management training should eliminate this and keep her on top of what she's really capable of doing.

117

On the other hand, *'job enrichment'* (also called development) means there'll be opportunities to learn new things that will most likely help her towards her next promotion.

Barbara's problem was similar. She kept having tasks added to her position without having any change in the level of position she was filling. This was either a job-description problem or (if she was being given more of the same tasks) a job-dumping problem. If her new responsibilities were becoming a regular part of her job, she should ask for her job description to be updated, first making sure she had the facts to show her boss about how the level of responsibility of her tasks had changed.

Overtime Overload

Betty's boss made her feel as if she was inadequate, because she didn't handle the job the same way her predecessor had done. It turned out that the other woman had voluntarily worked until eight o'clock every night without extra pay.

Don't fall for that one! She obtained a copy of her local overtime policy then talked to her boss, *'When I took this position I was told that the hours of work were eight to four and that there might be some overtime. I find that to get my work done, I have to work overtime almost every night. This isn't what I was led to expect. Am I required to work overtime every night? If so, I expect to be paid either overtime or time off in lieu of.'*

Janet also had an overtime problem. *'I had to start mentioning on Monday that they shouldn't expect me to work late Thursday night because I had made other plans. Otherwise they would expect me to be on call. I find I can't make plans any more.'* She should have a meeting with her boss to clarify when she is expected to work late.

Understaffed

How do you convince your employer that they need extra staff? Use facts. The facts are that:

- You've had to work overtime almost every night to take care of rush jobs *(supply time sheets to prove this)*.
- Work given to you by departments is getting out later every week *(give details)*.

118

- Mistakes are being made because you have to rush (*give details*).
- Morale is down (*give examples*) and
- You're hearing verbal complaints from people who've had to wait too long for their work *(give details)* - reports are late (*name which ones)*.

Remember, your boss has to justify to his or her supervisors why the department needs extra staff, so give him or her the ammunition needed to accomplish this. Don't keep attempting to cope and cope - you'll just get further behind and make mistakes.

Another approach to this problem, using the above information as back-up, is to recommend,

'I suggest you get someone in to look after my overtime work. You'll be paying me time-and-a-half for overtime and by that time of the day - I'm tired so can't give you my best work. On the other hand, if you hired a part-time employee, this person would be paid regular wages and would come to work fresh. This person could probably handle some of Sally's work, too, because she and I are often the only ones here at that time of the night. Between Sally and me, I'm sure there's enough work to have the person come in three to four hours every day. What do you think?'

The Disorganised Boss

Tanya voiced another common problem: *'My boss is disorganised and doesn't appear to know what's going on. I'm a very organised person. What should I do?'*

She'd ask him if there were any duties he would like to delegate to her so she could lighten his load. Or if she was feeling brave, she could ask him if he would like her to help him become more organised. If neither of these were possible, she had two choices. She could relax and tolerate the chaos or ask for a transfer to another position.

Too Many Bosses

Darlene had problems dealing with more than one boss. Quite often she had two top-priority things to do at the same time - for two

119

different people. She discussed the problem with the two supervisors, explaining her dilemma and asked *them* to make the decision. She shouldn't have to make that decision herself, unless they were absent and couldn't give their input.

Grace had this problem with a twist. She asked if this tactic would work when one boss was more senior than the other. Again, if the senior one gave her a new job, she should say, *'Brian asked me to do this job. Does your task take precedence over that one?'* Let *him* make the decision.

Job classification Inequities

Margaret asked, *'What if a female and male are doing essentially the same job and the males are being paid more? What can the woman do?'* She'd already confronted her manager and asked why this was happening. Her boss had sent in her job description and it had come back unchanged (in a lower classification than her male co-worker).

She asked for a personal interview, where she presented *all* the facts and written documentation to back up her claim and showed her boss the indisputable evidence that the two positions had the same level of responsibility. She has the right (by law) to fight for this equality. It's important for all workers to compare their jobs with those of others in the same department, especially if the staff is a mixture of men and women. In the past, women have been reluctant to do this. It's one of the main equal-rights and equal-opportunity issues facing government and businesses today.

However, an employee in this position should also be willing to listen to the employer's side of the story. There might be extenuating circumstances she isn't aware of. The other position may call for more experience or education than hers.

If you find you're underpaid and can't get your company to change the situation, the Human Rights and Equal Opportunities Commission will fight for you to make sure both of you (male and female) are paid the same salary for the same level of work.

What if you are having difficulty seeing the job descriptions of your co-workers? I don't understand why companies do this. It's important for employees to know the responsibilities of the workers around them, so they understand their company better. If you can't get the description from your supervisor or manager, ask your co-workers themselves for copies of their job descriptions. Explain that you need the information as a guide for updating your own description. (You're not lying - if your job description was completed more than two years ago - it's probably outdated.) Say that yours isn't accurate and you'd like to review an accurate one. Try it - it just might work.

You might also try talking to the people in the Human Resources Department directly. Hopefully, they have copies of the job descriptions for all positions in the company and may be willing to release this information - even if your boss won't.

Many women fear they might be fired if the *'make waves'* and ask for an accurate job description even though they're entitled to it. But your employer wouldn't dare fire you either for requesting an up-to-date job description or for pointing out that your job has been incorrectly classified. Make sure you document your struggle to obtain equality. In your place a man would almost certainly fight for an accurate description and classification.

Be careful that you describe your position correctly. If you're involved in updating your job description, use strong action verbs such as *'responsible for, in charge of, in control of, supervises,'* etc. (providing that's the case). For instance, one clerical job summary stated *'Is courteous and helpful to all visitors.'* In reality, this person had complete charge of a real estate office including supervision of a staff of three, setting appointments, preparing all documentation relating to home sales, receiving payments and the care of all confidential documents. When the job description was written and classified accurately, it was found that the position salary range went from $30,000 - $35,000 to $45,000 - $50,000 per annum.

You're now a supervisor!

You're excited, because you've finally been appointed to your first supervisory position! Read on to learn the kinds of unique problems you might face as a female supervisor.

Chapter Seven

Problems of female supervisors

Being a female boss

Many women won't admit it, but they have sexist attitudes of their own. These women seem able to take orders from male, but not from female supervisors. Unconsciously, they feel that only men should be supervisors. As a result, they question the ability of their female supervisors and make things difficult for them.

Have you ever reported to a female boss? Was she a good or bad supervisor? If she was inept as a supervisor - do you have any idea why? One of the major reasons why many women fail as supervisors is that they've never had any kind of supervisory training. These women are set up to fail by management, as is anyone else promoted into a supervisory role who does not have adequate training.

It's extremely important for women climbing the corporate ladder to obtain the right kind of supervisory training, preferably *before* they take their first supervisory position. If they're supervisors now, they owe it to themselves to get this training *whether their companies pay for it or not.* People who don't know how to act as supervisors appear unsure of themselves. Others lose respect for them and take advantage of them. It's not true that people are born knowing how to supervise.

Do you recall any situations where you or your co-workers sabotaged your female boss? Did you make her look even worse than she was? Sometimes the temptation to do this is over-whelming; but before you give in to this urge, ask yourself, *'What will I really be doing if I make her look bad?'* You will be making *all* existing and future female supervisors look bad.

When you're working for a female boss, it's your responsibility to help her look good. Why? This is because in most cases a woman who's promoted to a supervisory or management position is on trial. If she fails - this reflects on all the women who follow her. Every time you help a woman fail at her job, you hold back others who may be qualified - including yourself perhaps. If she doesn't make it, management is going to think twice before hiring another 'dud.' So without knowing it - you could be holding yourself back from future promotional opportunities.

If you do everything in your power to make your female supervisor look good, she'll most likely pull you along with her (faster than most male bosses). Start by explaining to her you understand the pressures she's under and that you're on her side. Tell her you want her to succeed and will do everything in your power to make her look good. For example, you may hear things from your peers that she'll never hear at her level, so keep her informed.

Tell a male boss the same thing (but be aware that this is *not* one of the games played in business - so he might be a little confused by your offer). Still, it's worth trying. What have you got to lose?

PROBLEMS OF FEMALE BOSSES

Un-cooperative staff

If you're a female boss and are having problems with your female subordinates, explain the situation to them. If you hear that someone's trying to sabotage you, be direct. Say, *'I really need your support and help and I notice that you're not co-operating. I'd like to know why.'*

Support staff (mainly women) normally go out of their way to keep their bosses (usually male) organised, on time and comfortable. They nurture their bosses (bringing them coffee, reminding them of appointments, opening and sorting their mail). But when a woman is promoted to the same supervisory position, the nurturing may stop unless she's on top of the situation. You'll have to let your staff know you expect the same kind of service the former male supervisor received.

Supervising older workers

Janet had a problem that at one time was rare, but occurs quite often now that young women are becoming more educated and able to take on supervisory roles at an earlier age. As a twenty-five-year-old college graduate, she was hired by a company to supervise her company's clerical division. She had four years' experience in an

124

office but wasn't prepared to supervise women almost twice her age that had an average of ten to fifteen years' office experience. They were openly hostile to her and did everything *but* co-operate.

When correcting a subordinate's behaviour, she needed to concentrate on the work-related behaviour (i.e.: sloppy reports) rather than on the subordinate's attitude. She'll also need to find ways to show she respected their experience and expertise. She'd learn about their career goals and demonstrate that she was willing to help them reach their goals.

Janet decided to invite Sarah, one of the less hostile women, into her office to discuss the problem. Sarah was honest. She admitted she had been surprised and disappointed when Janet had been 'hired off the street' as her supervisor. She had pictured someone her own age or older filling the position - possibly one of her own peer group or someone whose experience she felt would give her the 'right' to supervise. Instead, she found a woman the same age as her daughter in the role. She admitted that when Janet complimented her on a job well done - she felt patronised and when she corrected her behaviour or work - she became defensive.

Once these feelings were brought out into the open, the two women were able to start again. Janet now understood the reasons for Sarah's antagonism and could deal with it better. Sarah understood why she felt as she did and made an effort to change her attitude toward Janet.

Janet called a meeting with the rest of her staff to discuss the situation with them. She explained that she understood how they felt, what she needed from them and that she was counting on them to co-operate. She then asked each staff member, *'Can I count on you in the future?'* One employee, Julie appeared reluctant to make a commitment to her, so Janet knew she would have to watch her. Soon the woman's low productivity and poor quality of work made it necessary for Janet to take disciplinary steps to stop the unacceptable behaviour.

She again explained to Julie what she expected from her and what the consequences would be if she continued to produce sloppy work. Unfortunately, Julie never did accept Janet as her supervisor and continued doing sloppy work until Janet was forced to fire her.

Janet fared better with the other employees. When she noticed decided changes in their attitude and productivity, she thanked them for their understanding and co-operation.

Traditionally, society has taught us that the older woman - the mother or the aunt - knows more, so therefore is to be treated with deference and respect. Switching roles is disconcerting to both the young female supervisor (who's suddenly in the position of the 'mother') and the older female employee (who's now in the position of the 'daughter' seeking approval). These feelings are related to beliefs about power and who should have it. It's a situation with no set solutions that will work every time.

Supervising men

Barbara supervised a staff of three men. She was an engineer and the men were technologists. Her subordinates didn't seem to listen to her and insisted on doing things 'their' way. Fortunately, before taking the position, she had obtained proper supervisory training, which equipped her to act confidently. It became necessary to have a disciplinary interview with one of her male subordinates when he refused to do a task Barbara had assigned him.

This was a case of insubordination (a very serious problem) that could have led to the termination of the employee. She had a meeting with him defining the problem and placed a strong written warning on his file stating that he would be terminated if it happened again. She knew the importance of keeping her own supervisor up-to-date and he commended her on the competent way she had handled the touchy situation.

Could you do this if you were supervising men? If you're planning on climbing the ladder, it's a distinct possibility that you *will* be supervising and disciplining men in the future. Make sure you're prepared to do so.

Supervising former peers

What should you do on the first day on your new appointment as supervisor of staff that used to be your peers? You know that several of them applied for the same position, so know there will be some animosity towards you. You'll likely fail if you don't handle the first days or week properly. It's essential to remove any feelings of envy and jealousy of your new subordinates right away.

You'll need the co-operation of your manager. Before you became supervisor, he should have informed each of your peer group who were unsuccessful, why they didn't get the position and why you did. Then he should call a meeting where he would introduce you as their new supervisor. He'd explain that he expected their full co-operation and support. He'd then turn the meeting over to you and leave.

What do you do now that you're in charge of the meeting? Start by saying, *'I know that a few of you applied for and wanted my promotion. I can understand that you may feel upset that I got the position instead of you. However, the company chose me, so what we do from now on depends on how all of us work together. I need your support to handle my job properly. In return, I'll do everything I can to be a good supervisor. Can I count on your support?'*

Ask those present, one by one, to indicate to you whether you can rely on them: *'Marge - how about you, can I count on your support?' 'Dave?'* Cover every employee in the room, giving full eye contact when speaking with each one. If your staff make verbal commitments to you in front of witnesses, they're much more likely to co-operate in future.

Explain that you'll be having a meeting with each of them to learn more about their skills and abilities and that even though you worked with them in the past, you need to learn more about their responsibilities and tasks. You'll also be going over their job descriptions to make sure they're up-to-date and accurate for the work they're performing.

Before your meeting with each staff member, examine the person's personnel file. Explore their resume to learn about their responsibilities at former jobs, how much experience they've had and their formal education and training. Then examine past performance appraisals and carefully read over their job description. Then at the meeting, discuss your findings with them and update their job description if necessary.

At the initial meeting you noticed that Marge didn't seem to give the same assurance of co-operation as the rest of your staff. At her meeting, you'd say, *'Marge, at our first meeting, I detected some*

127

hesitancy when I asked for your co-operation. What can I do to make the situation a little easier for you?' If she still balks, you'll have to keep your eye on her. She might try to sabotage your efforts. If she does, you'll have to be on top of the situation and take immediate correctional action.

Boss Disciplines in public

'My boss keeps correcting my work and disciplining me in front of my co-workers and clients. He also calls me names and labels me instead of talking about what I did wrong.'

Aggressive bosses haven't learned one of the basic fundamentals of supervision. Subordinates can't be pushed into doing a good job; they have to be lead. A boss who disciplines employees publicly (or labels them rather than dealing with their behaviour) is bound to fail.

But what can you, as an employee, do? Tell him - that's what! If you work in a union environment, make sure a union representative is present to help with this bullying behaviour. Let your boss know what his behaviour is doing to you. This takes nerve, but most bosses will look up to you for having the courage to do it. For example, if your boss has disciplined you publicly, wait until he has calmed down and ask him for five minutes of his time. Start by saying, *'I have a problem and I need your help in solving it. Twice last week you disciplined me in front of my staff and clients. I felt very embarrassed and demoralised. In the future, could you please save such comments for times when we have some privacy?'* If the behaviour continues, you might have to add, *'I hope you understand that if you do this to me in the future, I'll simply walk away from you.'*

If your boss labels you, instead of talking about your unsuitable behaviour, discuss the matter with him privately. Say, *'I have a problem and I need your help in solving it. I find it difficult to handle the complaints about my work you've made lately. If you have a complaint, please correct my behaviour or work - but please don't call me names. I can't defend my actions when you call me names. Telling me that I made a mistake in setting up the marketing plan for the Carter account allows me to change my behaviour. The way it is now, I don't know how to improve my performance or what you really want of me. Can I count on you to do this for me?'*

If either of these behaviours continues, document your efforts to alleviate the problem and ask a union or employee relations person to help you deal with the problem.

Don't go to *his* boss and complain. If the situation doesn't change, put up with it while working for a transfer to another position in the company or leave for greener pastures. Whenever you feel your boss has removed all the pride and pleasure you get from your work - it's time to leave.

Aggressive female label

One seminar participant asked how she could handle a situation where, as a supervisor, she was regarded as aggressive - when she felt she was just standing up for her rights. She was a very forceful, self-assured individual and her tone of voice and her aggressive body language appeared to be the problem. By moderating her commands from *'I want you to do this'* into requests, *'I'd like you to ...'* she would leave her staff with a much more favourable impression and would likely gain their co-operation.

Several weeks after attending an assertiveness training class, a woman's boss accused her of being an aggressive female. Before obtaining her training, she'd been a very passive person who allowed her boss to dump more and more work on her without complaint. After her training, she realised that she had no choice but to object. She'd been warned at the training course, that she might run into resistance from others - especially those who'd walked all over her in the past. She understood that this was her boss's problem - not hers. Instead of caving in to his demands (as she had done in the past) she remained firm using facts to prove that he was overloading her with too many tasks.

Invades Privacy

Joyce's female manager kept interrupting her work with small talk, wanting to know all about her personal life. Joyce objected to this because she didn't want to talk about her personal life and found she was constantly falling behind in her work. When she objected about her work interruptions, she felt it caused hard feelings. I advised her to keep refusing, but as tactfully as possible by saying, *'I prefer to keep a strong division between my private and business life. I've found it's better for me.'* Further pressure from her boss could be regarded as aggressive behaviour that should be challenged, *'Why is my private life so important to you?'*

It's obvious that her female manager had not been given basic supervisory training, which would have advised her that employees should leave their personal lives at home and not to interfere with those of her staff unless it was affecting their productivity or behaviour.

The importance of obtaining proper supervisory training

If you're a supervisor and don't have adequate supervisory training - make that your top priority. The techniques aren't hard to learn and once you know the right way to do something, you'll feel more confident. If you're not a supervisor (but hope to become one soon) - don't wait until a supervisory position is available. Get the training first. It will give you an edge, when you're applying for a supervisory position. If your employer won't pay for this training, look upon it as an investment in your future and pay for it yourself.

Some participants in my intensive three-day supervisory training seminar have been in supervisory positions for years but have been given no supervisory training at all. As a result they've had to learn how to do their jobs through trial and error. How much easier it would have been, if they had received training either *before* commencing their supervisory responsibilities or shortly thereafter.

Supervisory training is crucial for men and women who wish to succeed in business. Although a first-line supervisory position is not necessarily on the path to the top, supervisors have an important function to perform. It's the first step towards management training, which is much more intensive. Unless you do your job well, your subordinates, your company and most of all *you* will look bad.

Read on to learn how you can be a good supervisor.

Chapter Eight

How to be a good supervisor

Essential supervisory responsibilities

In the workplace, anyone who is responsible for the actions of others is a supervisor, regardless of their title; supervisor, foreman/woman, manager, director, superintendent, vice-president or even president or CEO of a company. They all supervise others and therefore need training on how to do their jobs properly.

When I conduct my *'Dealing with difficult people'* seminars, I'm constantly bombarded by the problems staff have in the workplace. Initially I assumed that the major problems of employees would be those they had with clients - and secondly the ones they had with workmates. I was wrong. Over sixty percent of their problems came from the way their supervisors were treating them. It became obvious that these supervisors had not obtained even basic supervisory training. They made the following mistakes:

1. Disciplined their staff in front of workmates or clients.
2. Labelled staff's behaviour (stupid, dumb) or made sarcastic remarks, instead of trying to correct the actual behaviour of the staff member.
3. Didn't give recognition for a job well done.
4. Didn't back up their staff when dealing with customer complaints.
5. Didn't provide an effective, up-to-date job description with standards of performance for the tasks performed by their staff.
6. Didn't provide the necessary training to fill the gap between the job requirements and the employee's skills.
7. Conducted performance appraisals on staff members without proper job descriptions upon which to base their evaluation. (If the employee doesn't know what's expected of him/her and the supervisor doesn't know either - how can a fair evaluation of their performance be made?)
8. No set policy and procedure manuals available so the rules and regulations of the company are not clearly defined.
9. Harassed staff (either through bullying or sexual harassment).

10. Did nothing to improve the employee's interest in their jobs.
11. Were not available when their staff needed their help.
12. Wouldn't listen to their staff's suggestions about better ways to complete tasks.
13. Were perfectionists and expected everything to be done perfectly.
14. Had one set of company rules for staff – another for themselves. Bent rules when clients went over the head of front-line staff, causing embarrassment for staff members.
15. Allowed nepotism in the company. (Allowing friends and relatives to work in the same department – giving favouritism to friends and family members).

Being a good supervisor requires insight and empathy to understand why staff are behaving as they are. Unless you can put yourself in your staff's shoes and see things from their point of view - you'll fail. Be willing to listen to their suggestions. If their ideas won't work - explain why and be sure to give your staff credit where credit is due.

Has your company given you a supervisory title? Many men and women are given the title of supervisor, but their companies don't give them the authority to carry out the duties of their positions effectively. In reality - they're only 'lead hands' with little or no control over their subordinates' actions. To determine if yours is really a supervisor's position, ask yourself if your job has the four essential characteristics of supervision. Are you responsible for:

1. Delegating work to subordinates?
2. Checking subordinate's work?
3. Conducting performance appraisals?
4. Disciplining subordinates?
   The first two responsibilities are usually given to all people with the title 'supervisor' or 'foreman.' However, the second two often aren't. Insist on all four responsibilities (and the fifth if at all possible) are given to you. A fifth responsibility would be that of:
5. Hiring your own staff.

Let's look more closely at these duties:

132

Delegating work to subordinates

These are the actual tasks you give to your subordinates to complete. These should have standards of performance or competencies, so you can evaluate how well your staff completes assignments.

Checking subordinate's work

This is checking to see that the tasks you've delegated have been completed properly. You'll check the quality and quantity of how the task was performed and how long it took to complete them. This includes all tasks listed on a subordinate's job description. Was their work sufficient to meet the standards of performance set for each task?

Conducting performance appraisals

You should be the one who does the performance appraisal for all your subordinates - nobody else. Your boss shouldn't do them because s/he isn't directly responsible for the work of your subordinates. Your manager might review your findings to see if they're fair, but you should complete the appraisal on each employee you supervise.

Disciplining subordinates

Because ultimately your staff makes you look either good or bad, you need this control to correct production and/or behaviour problems. Because of the high number of wrongful dismissal claims, most companies now insist that a representative from their Human Resources Department be present if an employee is to be terminated. Unionised companies would have a representative present at any disciplinary meetings. Keep in mind that the main aim of discipline should be to improve your staff's productivity or behaviour problems - not to cause retaliation from the disciplined worker.

Hiring your own staff

This is a plus, but not always allowed by companies. Whenever possible have as much input as you can when hiring your staff. If you're 'out of sync' with a subordinate, you'll both find it very difficult to work as a team.

133

How does your supervisory position measure up? If you don't have the first four, you're in a very awkward position. You'll receive questionable respect from your subordinates and have little control over the outcome of their work. For example: Isabelle delegated a task to a subordinate and when she reviewed her work found it unsatisfactory. Isabelle took her employee aside to explain her dissatisfaction with her performance.

Her subordinate replied, *'So what? It looks good enough to me.'* Because Isabelle didn't have the authority to discipline the employee, she had no control over how her subordinate completed her work. She should ask for all four responsibilities so she can fully perform the duties of her position.

If your staff does a lousy job - who looks bad? You do! So, if your manager is doing the performance appraisals, explain, *'I've learned that one of my main responsibilities as a supervisor is preparing and conducting performance appraisals for my staff. I'd like to do them myself in the future. Do you have any objections?'* If you run into conflict, explain, *'If I don't have this right, you're removing some of my control and I need that control to do my job properly.'*

If your company sends you for supervisory training - keep in mind that top notch supervisory training includes the following:

The Role of the Supervisor

The transition between being an employee to being a supervisor involves many changes in attitude. As an employee, you probably only had to think about your own responsibilities. Now that you're a supervisor, you need to see every possibility from the company's point of view, rather than from an individual's point of view. The impact of decisions you make escalates as you rise higher in the company, as do the consequences. No longer are you only responsible for what you do, but for what your subordinates do as well. Unless you're a 'working supervisor,' there must be a distinct line between you and your subordinates.

Being a supervisor is very difficult. Managers are above giving you orders. Below are your staff members who can make you look good or bad. You're expected to co-operate with other supervisors, be a mediator in union disputes and implement policy with the help of other staff groups. You're caught in the middle, being pulled in every direction. Many supervisors have told me that they had no idea how much their responsibilities would change when they accepted their positions. Many compare the responsibilities to those of being a parent.

Leadership Styles

Do you think people are born as leaders? If you observed four or five two-year-olds playing together, you'd immediately pick out the ones who are leaders and those who are followers. However, this can change as a person grows up. The young leader may lose his or her ability to lead. No one will follow them because they've become bullies or haven't acquired the interpersonal skills necessary to lead. On the other hand, the original followers can learn the required skills and become a leader themselves.

When you were young, were you a leader or a follower? Have things changed now that you've grown up? Have you acquired the skills you'll need to lead your staff? A supervisor's leadership ability determines whether her staff will follow willingly or not. Bosses who prod (rather than lead) seldom obtain the best work from their staff. There are six basic leadership styles, ranging from authoritarian to participative. Supervisors are advised to seek as much employee involvement as possible. Here are alternative leadership approaches, starting with more authoritarian down to employee driven leadership:

1. Supervisor makes the decision and announces it. For instance, if there's a rule or regulation your company wishes you to impose - you would lead using a Theory X method (authoritarian style of leadership) by saying, *'This is how it's going to be done.'* There's no flexibility in this approach and no input from the employees.
2. Supervisor 'sells' the decision. The supervisor explains why the rule or regulation is necessary.
3. Supervisor presents ideas and invites questions. The supervisor allows employees to ask questions about the new rule or regulation.

4. Supervisor presents a tentative decision subject to change. The supervisor listens to suggestions of staff, but still makes the final decision.
5. Supervisor presents the problem, gets suggestions then makes the decision. The supervisor does not suggest a solution to the staff, but still makes the final decision.
6. Supervisor defines the limits and requests the group to make the decision. The supervisor says to employees, *'Here's a problem – you're on your own as to how you solve it. Let me know if you need help.'* This is a strong Theory Y example (employee driven style of leadership).

Delegation

This can be a difficult task for a woman who's been taking orders most of her life. Most supervisors don't understand the delegation process. As a supervisor, when you delegate a task to an employee, you can't divorce yourself from the task. You can't say, *'I told Sally to do that and she obviously didn't do it correctly.'* You're saying that Sally looks bad. Wrong. You both look bad! (That's how employees can sabotage their bosses.) Your job as a supervisor is to obtain the best performance from your employees, to challenge them, develop their talents and abilities and see that they've complete their delegated tasks properly.

Also important, is learning to give tasks to the right person at the right level, so your company spends its money well. For example: Many personal assistants hate making coffee. As her supervisor, you decide that you'll take your turn making coffee. Your manager sees you doing this and questions you about it: *'I saw you making coffee the other day - how come you're doing that?'*

You explain: *'My personal assistant really doesn't want to get stuck with that chore all the time - so I do my share of coffee making.'* The manager then exclaims, *'I'm paying you thirty-five dollars an hour. You shouldn't be spending your valuable time making coffee!'*

When you see this issue from management's or the owner's point of view - it makes sense. Why pay a supervisor's salary for those ten minutes, when a lower-paid employee was available. The person who's paid the least should do these menial kinds of tasks and those duties should be outlined in their job description. All tasks of your subordinates should be examined to see if someone receiving less pay should be doing the task.

Meeting Skills

Most supervisors spend a considerable portion of their time in meetings, many of which they chair themselves. Unless meetings are conducted correctly, they can turn out to be time-wasters for everyone involved. Learn how to chair a meeting correctly and handle problem attendees.

Motivation

Motivating employees to be productive and to use all their talents and abilities is one of management's biggest challenges. Supervisors need to find 'the hot button' of an employee with low productivity so they can utilise their unique talents and abilities. High achievers need to be constantly stimulated and allowed to develop their talents or they'll simply leave for a company that will allow them to do so. However, some employees are almost impossible to motivate except to threaten them with the loss of their job unless their productivity improves.

Time Management

This is important - no matter what position you hold. However, because you're now worth more money per hour, it costs your company more if you waste time and if you can't manage your own time - how can you utilise the time of your subordinates effectively?

Problem Solving and Decision-Making

People often spend time spinning their wheels because they're trying to solve the wrong problem. They spend hours working on a particular problem, instead of standing back from it to determine whether they're tackling the real problem. Many women excel at creative problem solving because they're very creative during brainstorming. Make use of that talent.

Interpersonal Skills

Many seminars and workshops are offered on this topic because management realises the importance of good communication skills at all levels of business. Training normally covers communication skills such as; speaking, listening, writing, reading body language and understanding why you and others behave the way you do.

Employment Interviewing

If you have the responsibility of choosing your staff, training in interviewing will help you to write advertisements, screen applications, prepare for an interview and determine what questions to ask on the interview (as well as what illegal interview questions you should avoid). This training also emphasises the importance of proper reference checking and gives guidance on how to choose the best person for the position. Other interviewing tasks would involve job description writing, performance appraisals and disciplinary interviews.

Training and Development

Often the person you hire does not meet all the requirements of the position. Many companies place the responsibility on supervisors to fill that gap using training techniques that will lock-in the training. Development is achieved when employees are given new kinds of assignments or placed in acting positions.

Employee Discipline

Not only do most new supervisors (and even seasoned ones) hate disciplining their subordinates, but especially hate having to fire a subordinate. Unfortunately, the majority of supervisors bring out the worst (rather than the best) in their employees, simply because they use ineffective tactics to correct the behaviour or performance of their subordinates. Instead of gaining the employee's co-operation, better behaviour and productivity - many just invite retaliation. There are some hard and fast rules to discipline (including laws which protect employees).

You can learn more about these supervisory responsibilities by obtaining my books:

Survival Skills for Supervisors and Managers and *Easy Come – Hard to Go: The art of hiring, disciplining and firing employees.*

Socialising with your staff

You've just been promoted and now supervise your former peers. How do you feel about socialising with your subordinates away from the work setting? Supervisors are encouraged to keep their business and private lives completely separate. If you're going to socialise with people you supervise, never discuss business while socialising. You're no longer a 'buddy' - you're a supervisor, with a totally different role to fulfil. Moreover, if you socialise with only two out of your five subordinates, the other three may think you're showing favouritism to the chosen two. However, you might wish to socialise with all your staff by having a departmental barbeque or Christmas party. That's acceptable.

How about socialising with your new peer group (other supervisors)? That's different. It's fine to socialise with them because you'll keep the 'old boy's network' going and learn a lot through this grapevine.

Supervisory problems:

Problem: *'I give indirect supervision to a staff of three. They do sloppy work, but I can't discipline them. My boss does it.'*

Response: This problem would not occur if you had the full responsibilities of a supervisor. Technically, you're in a 'lead hand' position. Approach your boss and explain to him or her, the kinds of problems this lack of control creates and ask either to be given the full supervisory responsibility or to have the three employees report directly to your boss. S/he will then delegate and check their work as well as disciplining the staff.

Problem: *'I'm a supervisor, but I've been told I don't have the right to promote the person I think should be promoted. I had two people I was considering for a promotion and I chose the one I felt was best qualified, but my manager overruled my decision.'*

Response: Use facts to prove why your decision was the best one and be willing to stand behind your decision. Because you're closer to these employees, you know things your boss doesn't. Use these facts to explain your point of view.

Also ask yourself whether it's a 'political' promotion. You may have to bite the bullet and give in, because your boss has control over what you do and you'll have to listen to his or her wishes. But do have your say first, before giving in.

Problem: Your staff resents the fact that you get credit for their ideas. They feel that if they do all the legwork and provide all the background information, they should get the credit.

Response: According to Rule #15 of the games played in business (explained in Chapter 3) a supervisor has a right to do this. However, in my supervisory classes I encourage participants to give credit where credit is due. Otherwise they're de-motivating their staff, rather than motivating them. Supervisors will obtain more productivity from their subordinates if they encourage them to come forward with new ideas and by giving credit for useful contributions.

Problem: *'I want to promote one of my female staff into a supervisory role but my company refuses to give her supervisory training.'*

Response: Before speaking to the employee, make sure that your company is not refusing her the training because she's a woman. If they provide supervisory training for men, but not women, they're breaking the rules of your Equal Opportunity Act. However, if your company simply doesn't have the budget to provide the training to any supervisor, explain the company situation to the employee.

Do emphasise the importance to her of obtaining supervisory training. You might point out that she owes it to herself to help herself succeed, even if her company won't. Most educational costs are tax deductible. It should also be kept in mind that a small financial investment now will earn her not only a promotion, but future income as well.

Problem: *'I never hear about the 98% of my tasks that I do right, only about the 2% of tasks that I do wrong. Why doesn't my boss recognise what I'm doing right? It's just too frustrating!'*

Response: Nobody likes to be told they or their work are unacceptable and if recognition for good work is not given, employees simply stop trying. Talk to your boss and explain how upsetting it is to only hear about what you've done wrong and nothing about what you've done right. High on all employees' lists of motivators is that their supervisors give them credit where credit was due and concentrate on the good work they'd done. And when correcting behaviour, instead of stating *'You made a mistake.'* Or, *'You didn't do that right!'* (Which just puts the staff member on the defensive) these supervisors should correct unacceptable work by saying, *'In the future I'd like you to do it this way.'* Remember this when you're a supervisor.

Problem: *'Some day, I want to be a supervisor myself, but my boss is very reluctant to give me any kind of help in getting there. It's almost as if he's afraid that I might want his job. Of course, I do, but that shouldn't stop him from helping me develop so I'm ready for the next step up!'*

Response: You're right - your supervisor is probably afraid that you're getting too good. You've become what I call a 'heel nipper.' Some supervisors fear that their subordinates are becoming too competent, so hold them back. However, unless someone is nipping at their heels and is equipped to take over their positions - they won't be promoted to higher positions themselves. All supervisors should have one or two subordinates ready to take over their positions.

One of a supervisor's responsibilities is to develop the talents and abilities of his or her staff so they're ready for their next promotion. If your boss isn't providing this opportunity, speak to a Human Resources representative or ask for a lateral move where you will be working under a more willing supervisor.

Problem: *'I often feel as if I'm speaking a different language than men. They seem to misunderstand me so often.'*

Response: Some differences between men and women are the result of conditioning. Others appear to be inherited. Women need to make a determined effort to learn 'male language.' I always assumed that the same word meant the same thing to both men and women, but my research indicates that this is not so. For example, in a social gathering of both men and women, I heard a woman in the group discussing her career aspirations. She stated that a job she was considering would be a real challenge.

The man she was with, asked her why she was even considering the position. She again stated, *'As I explained, it'll be a real challenge.'*

'Well then, turn it down!' he repeated.

They discussed the issue for a while but ended up in an argument. The rest of us sat by, wondering what the problem was. It suddenly became apparent to me that they were discussing different things. To clarify matters, I asked each of them to explain to me what the word 'challenge' meant to them.

The woman explained that the word 'challenge' meant that something was exciting, that it gave her a chance to prove herself, to stretch, to reach her full potential (a very positive meaning).

Her male partner felt that the word 'challenge' meant someone was standing in his way, keeping him from obtaining what he wanted. He felt that, if challenged, he would prepare to do 'battle' to overcome the obstruction.

This revelation started the group trying to think of words that meant different things to men and women. We were able to come up with a few and I'm constantly seeking others. Two examples follow.

Macho: To a man it suggests a strong, decisive leader, worthy of respect - a trendsetter and role model. To a woman this means a chauvinistic man who thinks he's 'God's gift to women.' It may carry connotations of small- or narrow-mindedness and vanity.

Gentle: To a man it suggests someone mentally weak, soft and wish-washy, an indecisive 'wimp,' someone who can be pushed around by others, is passive and perhaps physically weak as well. To a woman this suggests someone tender, empathetic and in tune with others - someone who does not take advantage of others but is dependable, unassuming, trustworthy and kind.

There are many words we use very day that have these different meanings for men and women. If you find yourself in a situation, where you think the word you're using is being misinterpreted - use paraphrasing to confirm the meaning.

A high degree of confidence is required to perform all the many tasks and take on the responsibilities of a supervisor. Confidence is gained by doing things that constantly boost your self-esteem and self-confidence levels. How would you rate your self-confidence level? Find out how to keep your self-confidence high by reading the next chapter.

Chapter Nine

How to raise your self-confidence

We all want to feel good about ourselves, but some people feel they have to succeed in their careers *before* they can feel good about themselves. Our self-confidence - or lack of it - determines our behaviour. It can make us passive and socially compliant - sacrificing our own needs and become a doormat. It can make us aggressive - satisfying our own needs at the cost of hurting others and inviting retaliation. Or it can make us nicely assertive - with realistic concern for ourselves but also for the needs and feelings of those around us. If others *'walk all over us'* or we alienate others by our behaviour, our chances of success will be harmed in both cases.

To change our approach to others, we may need to change our views about ourselves.

Behaviour styles

Our behaviour reveals a great deal about our attitudes both towards ourselves and towards others. There are three basic types of behaviour and three more where others use manipulation to try to make us do what we don't want to do. We'll start with the basic three, passive, aggressive and assertive.

Passive Behaviour

Passive people seldom express their own wants and needs and usually give in to the demands and wants of others. They're reluctant to defend their rights and stand up for themselves. Their behaviour portrays that they don't respect themselves.

Aggressive Behaviour

Aggressive people show little respect for the needs and wants of others. They expect things to be done their way - or not at all. They have difficulty placing themselves in the shoes of others (lack empathy). They take advantage of others. The hair will rise on the back of your neck when these people are around and you will be ready to protect yourself.

Assertive Behaviour

Assertive behaviour is the healthiest behaviour of all. Assertive people show by their attitude to others, that they respect themselves. They're not afraid to express their needs to others and are willing to defend their rights. On the other hand, they allow others to express their needs and defend their rights as well.

Nobody can force another to give up his or her rights. The only person who can give up those rights is the one who owns them. Unless it's part of the normal give-and-take in relationships, we become less of a person if we give up our rights to someone else. Assertive people practice this.

Many women still follow the traditional behaviour of their mothers and grandmothers, who were taught that passive behaviour was the normal and accepted behaviour for women. Those who compete or become too powerful (an un-feminine trait according to traditionalists) are made to believe that they're acting aggressively. In reality, they're acting assertively. Women who succeed in business have had to unlearn their traditional passivity in order to be more assertive. A few have overcompensated, have gone to the other extreme and have become aggressive.

Next, we'll discuss the sub-categories. These people use manipulation to try to get others to do something they don't want to do:

Passive Resistance

Passive-resistant types are passive people who are trying to be more assertive. They mutter and sigh a lot and play manipulative games to get their way. They have not learned to ask for what they want in an up-front manner. Such manipulative plays as passive-resistance (complaining, whining, dragging your feet but never directly stating your grievance to others) are ineffective and create bad feelings.

Indirect Aggression

These people are somewhere between assertive and aggressive. They use such subtle, under-handed methods to get their way such as sabotage, sarcasm, the silent treatment and gossip, using manipulative games, instead of acting assertively. For instance:

Don: *'My wife wants me to clean the basement this weekend. I'm going to give it a stab, but I won't clean it to her standards. Then maybe she won't expect me to do that job again.'* (Sabotage).

Jane: *'I see you finally made the decision to get your hair cut in a style that suits you.'* (Sarcasm).

Linda hadn't spoken to her co-worker Bruce for four days following an argument. They hadn't resolved the issue and Bill had tried several times to get her to talk about the problem - she refused. (The Silent Treatment).

Jill: *'Did you hear about Carmen's husband ... He was picked up for drunk driving last night.'* (Gossip).

Passive-aggressive

As most of us grow up, we're faced with restrictions that are normal and necessary. Passive/aggressive people have a pathological reaction to authority and those they perceive are in positions of authority. They channel their aggression into passive behaviour by slowing down the efforts of others, stonewall progress and are very hard to detect. Others often feel frustrated when dealing with them, but don't always understand why.

Those with passive-aggressive personalities have often been controlled excessively, so they learn to control others without confrontation. They love the thrill of insubordination and it sometimes doesn't matter if they win - as long as it appears that their opponents loose. They love to play win-lose games and put something over on others.

They use excuses such as: *'It's not my fault this didn't work; it's yours.'* They show frequent signs of being helpless - the simplest matter seems beyond their comprehension. They provoke a feeling of defensiveness when dealing with others. Most tasks are performed late - or not at all. When prodded, they become argumentative. They're backstabbers, gossipers and are often so good at it, that others believe their falsehoods.

Most people display the above signs at one time or another. However, if this develops into their normal behaviour, these people are likely passive-aggressive and others will have to remain on guard

145

when dealing with them. Confront them using facts when you *'catch them in the act.'* Make sure they understand the consequences of their actions. Say, *'If this happens again, I'll have to ...'*

Some serious passive/aggressives have criminal tendencies. These people get a thrill out of speeding, of drinking and driving - and getting away with it. In some, this tendency keeps accelerating, because they require higher and higher levels of danger, thrills and excitement to keep them appeased.

Let's look at the three major types of behaviour in more detail.

Passive behaviour

Passive people and those who use passive-resistance often feel:

* Angry (because they feel others take advantage of them);
* Frustrated (because they seldom get their way);
* Withdrawn and defeated (because they feel they have nothing to say, so nobody listens to them);
* Inferior (because they lack self-esteem and self-confidence);
* Anxious and insecure (because they feel they have little control over their lives);
* Inadequate (because they feel others are better than they).

These feelings may make them irritable, but they often lack the courage to acknowledge their feelings of fear and inadequacy, by pretending that everything's all right. They:

* Don't know how to increase their self-confidence;
* The negative feedback they invite often reinforces their poor self-image;
* Seldom attempt new things;
* Don't take risks because they're afraid they'll fail;
* Don't know how to handle failure;
* Put themselves down;
* Have difficulty accepting even the simplest compliment;
* Tend to underestimate the value of what they do;
* Seem to lack energy and zest because they're usually doing things that others want them to do, rather than things they would choose to do;
* Believe that while you may be 'okay' - they're 'not okay.'

Aggressive behaviour

Aggressive and indirectly aggressive people often feel:

- Powerful (in the short run because they enjoy seeing people scurry and rush to carry out their orders);
- Guilty (in the long run, because they know they alienate people and sense that they're taking advantage of others);
- Threatened (by those they perceive as 'better' than they).

These feelings may impel them to constantly brag about how good, how intelligent or how strong they are and to try to make themselves feel important by putting others down. They:

- Are always right;
- Seem to believe the only ideas worth listening to are their own;
- Frequently blame others for things that go wrong;
- May have a high energy level, but usually their energies are geared in the wrong direction, towards destructive rather than constructive activities;
- Are experts at passing the buck;
- Are often isolated (having alienated everyone around them);
- Believe they're 'okay' - but that you're 'not okay.'

Assertive behaviour

Assertive people often feel:

- Optimistic (because they approach new tasks and ideas with a positive rather than a negative attitude);
- Calm (because they're at peace with themselves and others);
- Enthusiastic (because they expect to succeed);
- Satisfied (because they know where they're going and how they're going to get there. They usually attain their goals);
- In control (because they seldom have mood swings that affect their communication with and behaviour towards others);
- Self-confident (because they feel they can reach their goals without stealing ideas from others or climbing over others).

These people are able to be honest and direct. They:

147

- Are confident enough to take risks when necessary, but they know their limitations;
- Are not overwhelmed when they don't succeed at something;
- Are not afraid to acknowledge their own failings or feelings about what others' behaviour is doing to them;
- Are able to respect other people and to accept respect in return;
- Usually have lots of energy, which they're able to channel in the right direction;
- Feel that they're 'okay,' - and that you're 'okay' too.

Consequences of the main behavioural styles

It's important to know what each kind of behaviour does to those around you and how they're likely to react to you, if you use that behavioural style.

Passive Behaviour: often brings out other people's aggressive tendencies and they don't like the resulting guilt feelings. For example, suppose you have to work overtime unexpectedly. Jane (another mother with a child in day-care) picks up your daughter and looks after her until you come home. Lately you've had considerable overtime. Jane has never asked for the same favour in return. You've offered to babysit her children in the evenings or weekends, but Jane hasn't taken you up on this. She's a very passive person who lets people take advantage of her and you feel guilty because you feel you're acting aggressively. So, to alleviate these guilt feelings, you make alternative child-care arrangements and don't have much contact with Jane any more.

Jane alienated your friendship by allowing you to take advantage of her (which was exactly the opposite of what she intended). Passive people such as Jane must realise what they do to others and stop acting so passively! She may believe she's pleasing you by never asking for a favour in return. The last thing she wants to do is alienate you, but that's exactly what she does.

Passive behaviour, therefore, may make other people feel:

- Angry (because they wish you'd ask for what you need and make decisions for yourself);

148

- Frustrated and impatient (because it bothers them when you refuse all their attempts to help or to even things up);
- Threatened (because your negative attitude makes it difficult for them to maintain their own positive thinking);
- Disrespectful (because you don't respect yourself enough to stand up for what you believe in).

Aggressive Behaviour may make the people around you feel:

- Threatened and angry (because you try to make yourself look good by attacking them and putting them down);
- Frustrated (because they have to expend so much energy just defending themselves from your abuse);
- Resentful (because you've acquired power over them by unfair means);
- Defensive (because they expect you to attack);
- Hurt (by your sarcasm, silent treatment and putdowns);
- Humiliated (because you correct them and/or try to make them look foolish in front of others).

Assertive Behaviour may make the people around you feel:

- Positive (because your positive, confident attitude is infectious);
- Safe (because they trust you);
- Satisfied (because you're capable of noticing *their* good points as well as your own);
- Co-operative (because you know how to make them feel good about themselves, so they enjoy working with you);
- Respected (because you're willing to listen to their views, to negotiate and don't have to have things go your way all the time);
- Energetic (because there are no games being played and they're able to use their energy constructively).
- Envious (because they wish they could be more like you).

Do passive people usually achieve their goals? No, because they seldom have goals in the first place.

Do aggressive people usually achieve their goals? Sometimes in the short run, but they invite retaliation in the long run.

149

Do assertive people usually achieve their goals? Yes. Their aim is not to win at others' expense but to achieve their goals by finding solutions that benefit everyone.

Manipulation

Men and women often get their way by manipulating others. Manipulation is closely related to game playing. If you're an obvious manipulator or game player, people won't trust you. Perhaps you use manipulative tactics or play games without realising it. If you think this could be the case, the book *Games People Play*, by Eric Berne, may help you identify your games or read my book *'Dealing with Difficult People* that has an entire chapter explaining the 115 ways people try to manipulate others and how to handle those situations.

Confidence in speaking

Those who lack self-confidence may tremble when they even think about speaking in public. Most supervisors and managers have to make group presentations, so verbal fluency is essential for them to progress in business. In order to say what they want to say, they need to feel assertive enough to express their points of view. If they aren't sure what they want to say, it will show in their speaking style. If they freeze up, they're in trouble.

Body language is also important. Men's voices tend to deepen when they're nervous; women's become shrill or breathless. Many women hunch over when they're nervous, which reduces their lung capacity and makes it harder to project their voices. A man is more likely to assume a defiant posture - with shoulders straight, chest out, head up - when they're nervous. This expands their chest and gives their voices more volume. Try using your diaphragm if you have to project your voice.

Whenever we feel anxious or uneasy, we naturally tend to comfort ourselves by rubbing, patting or scratching ourselves. When we interact with others and feel uncomfortable, we'll break eye contact with them. So if you're making a speech, make eye contact with your audience, even if you're very uncomfortable.

When making public presentations women often appear tense, by *'pulling all their ends in'* as though trying to take up as little space as possible. Their shoulders and arms may appear stiff. Their hands may flutter to their faces when they're not sure of a point. Raised eyebrows and a forward-leaning posture suggest that they're looking for approval. The whole body is asking, *'Do you like what I'm saying?'*

Such women rely heavily on qualifying phrases, like, *'I guess ... I feel ... I believe ... or I think ...'* and end sentences with a question. For example, *'Wouldn't that be a good idea?'* Again, they appear to be seeking approval. This sort of presentation suggests uncertainty and indecisiveness.

If this describes you, try using a tape recorder to check your voice pattern - or better yet - use a video camera to identify areas that require improvement. Ask friends to assess your speeches. Practice until you *know* you're going to do a good job. Self-confidence is half the battle when giving a presentation. (The other half is to be properly prepared, with facts to back up your views.)

Self-sabotage

Sometimes we fail to get ahead because - without realising it - we sabotage ourselves. There's a 'little twerp' inside of all of us who asks maliciously, *'Who do you think you are?'* and questions our every action. When these doubts take over, they cause us to focus on some little thing we've done wrong that blocks out the good feelings we've gained from a job well done.

Or we dwell on our disadvantages, saying: *'If only I were younger, older, thinner, more beautiful, smarter, a better dresser, could talk better, sing better, dance better.'* Or: *'I should have stayed at school and obtained my degree'; 'I should have made a job change years ago;' 'I should have taken that promotion when it was offered to me!'* Don't *'if only'* or *'should'* on yourself! If you focus on the negatives in life, instead of remembering the good things you've done and may still do - you're letting yourself down.

At the same time, it may not be enough to consciously aim for a positive attitude if you're held back by fear. If you can identify the fears that are holding you back, you can find ways of dealing with them.

151

Fear of Success

The reasons for self-sabotaging behaviour can be quite complex. Perhaps you suspect that if you take risks and become successful, you might somehow lose the love of people who are important to you. Men regard their work as a duty, so do not assume that their wives will withhold love if they're taxed by the demands of their work. They don't assume, either, that their wives will be jealous of their success.

But most women are not convinced that they're owed unwavering love by a husband who may be inconvenienced or challenged by their work in the same way. Such women may be afraid to succeed. This is often a subconscious fear and the things they do to sabotage themselves are well camouflaged. Analyse your thoughts and behaviour to see if any of the following are happening to you.

1. Do you think you'll be seen as less feminine if you succeed? Successful females often appear to be far more competitive than the average woman. You may feel uncomfortable in this role or think men who feel intimidated by successful women might give you putdowns you couldn't handle.
2. Do you think you'll have to choose between being successful in a career and finding a spouse or mate? Or that if you're successful, you may lose the mate you already have? You may feel you can have one or the other (a mate or success) but not both.
3. Do you worry that if you choose to start climbing, you'll feel obliged to keep climbing until you overreach yourself and fail? You'd hate to fail, which you may think would be worse than not trying in the first place.

Fear of Failure

Women often turn down excellent opportunities and are not sure why they've done so. If you face this possibility, ask yourself, *'Why am I not taking this opportunity? Is fear of failure holding me back? Or is it lack of money, connections, time or child care?'* Learn to analyse why you're being your own worst enemy.

Fear of failure can convince you that you're incapable of handling more responsibility. It encourages you to think of every situation in which you couldn't possibly measure up and to turn down promotions because of those fears. If you *do* accept the position without dealing with those negative feelings - you're probably setting yourself up to fail. Keep in mind that you're capable of far more than you think. Never take a promotion to a position in which you know every aspect of the job. If you do - you're already overqualified for the position. All promotional opportunities should leave you room to grow and learn while on the job or through additional training.

Guilt

Guilt is hard to turn off. For example, Georgina went on short business trips to other cities. On one occasion she realised she was feeling uneasy. She thought, *'Why am I here, alone - and not with my family? I miss, need and want my husband and kids.'* She was ashamed of those feelings, so she altered them by turning them around to, *'My husband and kids miss, need and want me and right now I'm letting them down.'* She felt guilty that her family could not always come first with her. She'd been conditioned to believe that this was her role. To change her outlook, she assessed her guilt feelings, realised what had caused them, dealt with them then turned them off as not being realistic.

Learning to take risks

Webster's New World Dictionary defines the word *'risk'* as *'the chance of injury, damage or loss.'* It takes courage to take risks - but life without risk is very mundane and boring. Nothing ventured, nothing gained. Some fear not being able to *'pull it off'* - that they'll fail. They've been taught that failure's a bad thing, so in taking risks they're facing the possibility of ending up with not one, but two bad things; failure at what they've attempted to do and the added burden of lowered self-esteem.

Often racehorses win only by a *'nose.'* Why do we assume that we can't just win by a nose at what we attempt? We really don't have to be that much better than everyone else - just a *'nose'* better. To think otherwise, means we're expecting ourselves to be super-human.

153

Thank of things you don't do well. How do you know you don't do those things well? Perhaps you think you're not good at sports, but when was the last time you tested your abilities in this area? Are you letting a failure you had as a child or teenager limit your adult life needlessly?

Let's say that as a child you spilled your milk, tripped often, bumped into furniture and dropped things. You were never able to forget these 'failings' because you were reminded of them again and again by your parents, siblings and friends, until you began to believe you were as 'awkward' as they said you were. This then became a self-fulfilling prophecy. Thereafter, whenever you attempted something that took dexterity or co-ordination, you didn't bother trying, because your old negative tapes that said you were clumsy kept playing in your brain. You simply decided that you still couldn't do it and didn't even give it a try.

Analyse yourself. Do you have any negative tapes buzzing around in your brain that may be stopping you from trying something new? Test your abilities. Perhaps you're more capable than the negative tapes in your subconscious say you are.

I always approach new things with an open mind. I think, *'I've never tried this before, but I'll try my best.'* If I don't do well at it (and I know I've given it my best try) I've learned that this is something I really don't do well and I can go on to something else. If I *do* succeed at the task, the positive results usually spur me on to try other new things. With this positive approach, I find that I succeed in about three out of every five things I attempt - and the ratio is improving.

Do you let yourself feel that you have 'failed' at something when you've given your best effort? Why not think of it as being a learning experience. Take the word 'failure' out of your vocabulary. You can't be good at everything! If you think you have to be - you're bound to spend most of your life in misery. If you're holding off taking action because you're afraid to take the risk - do the following:

1. Define as closely as possible what you think the risk is.
2. Determine what you could **gain** emotionally and physically by making the attempt.

154

3. Determine what you could *lose* emotionally and physically by making the attempt.
4. Try to ascertain if you need more information before taking the risk. Where and from whom would you obtain this information?
5. What's the *best* thing that could happen if you took the chance and attempted it?
6. What's the *worst* thing that could happen if you took the chance and attempted it?
7. How could you lessen the risk?
8. Is it now worth taking the risk?

Do you over- or under-emphasise the consequences of everything you do? Have you hurt others in the past by acting too soon, with too little information? By analysing what your actions will do to others or how it will affect other projects, you'll be less likely to goof again.

Accepting compliments

Do you have trouble fielding compliments? When someone makes favourable comments about your outfit, do you find yourself replying, *'Oh, this old rag?'* We often discount or refuse to accept another's kind words. If you deserve a compliment, learn how to accept it with grace. If you can't accept it, what are you telling the person who pays you the compliment? That's right - you're calling them a liar or a poor judge of character. You're giving *them* a putdown. After all, they meant their comment to make *you* feel better, not to make *them* feel worse. You'll likely receive few compliments from that person in the future and we all need authentic praise to survive. The only compliments you should discount are 'marshmallows.' These are sickly sweet, manipulative remarks that simply aren't true or grossly exaggerate the truth.

How to increase self-esteem

If your self-image is drooping, change your life by attending a good assertiveness-training class. Ask around, check course outlines and attend one that you think will meet your particular needs. The most important assertive quality you can possess is that of being a positive thinker.

Positive Thinkers believe they will succeed because ...
Negative Thinkers believe they will fail because ...

Positive thinkers have taken the time to look at themselves objectively. They know what they do well and find as many opportunities to exercise their talents as possible. To do so, gives them good feelings about themselves. They're also aware of things they don't do well, but instead of sweeping this knowledge under the rug - they do something to improve their abilities.

You can help yourself become a positive thinker by doing the following:

1. Make a list of people you associate with on a regular basis. Make three headings:

    a) Positive thinkers
    b) Negative thinkers
    c) Those who are right in the middle. (Don't opt out by having too many people in this category.)

2. Determine the percentage of time you spend with each person. For instance, if you spend seven hours a day with four different people at work, you'll probably spend about twenty percent with each of them during the week. (You'll end up with a total well over 100 percent, but don't worry about that.)

3. Determine whether you're spending more time with positive- or negative-thinking people.

4. Now rate yourself. Are you basically a positive or negative thinker?

To help you with question 4, ask yourself these questions (the more 'yes' answers you have the better):

Answer: Yes or No:

a) Do you think of yourself as happy?
b) Are you surprised when a friend lets you down?
c) When you think back over the past few months, do you tend to remember your little successes before your failures and setbacks?
d) If you made a list of your ten favourite people, would you be on it?
e) Do you feel comfortable making yourself the butt of your own jokes?

f) When the unexpected forces you to change your plans, are you quick to spot the hidden advantages in the new situation?

g) When you catch a stranger staring at you, do you decide it's because s/he finds you attractive?

h) Do you like most of the people you meet?

i) When you think about the next year, do you tend to think you'll be better off than you are now?

j) Do you often stop to admire things of beauty or interest?

k) When someone finds fault with you for something you've done, can you tell the difference between useful (positive) criticism and the kind of griping that is better ignored?

l) Do you praise your best friend more often than you criticise him or her?

Do you spend too much time with negative thinking people? If so, you may have to reduce the time you spend with them, so you can either become a positive thinker or help yourself to stay one. If you work in an environment where you're forced to deal with negative-thinking people, it's essential for you to spend your time *away from work* with positive-thinking friends and family.

One participant in my *'Create a Positive Image'* seminar wrote to me afterwards to describe what she did to change the people she worked with (including herself) from negative to positive thinkers. When she arrived back at work after attending my seminar, she asked her co-workers to help her become a more positive-thinking person. She asked them to remind her every time they caught her using negative thinking.

Oddly enough, this worked for the entire group. They began catching each other when using negative thinking. This was so apparent to others, that about a month later, their boss called a staff meeting at which he said, *'I don't know what you're doing differently - but please keep it up!'* Help co-workers, friends and family by using this technique or you could ask them if they'd like you to help them be more positive thinkers.

If you're presently unemployed, it can be difficult to think positively, even if this is your normal frame of mind. I've advised people who attend my *'Get that Job!'* seminar that their attitude, (positive or negative) has a direct bearing on whether they're hired or not.

Employers are looking for positive thinkers and given the choice, wouldn't you too?

Positive thinking requires imagination, the ability to visualise succeeding and the belief that you can do it! If you expect to fail - you will. If you expect to succeed and work hard to achieve your goal - your chances of success are good.

How do you let people know you're a positive thinker?

- Let your clothing, appearance, posture and even the gleam in your eyes tell people you like and respect yourself.
- Try to associate with other positive thinkers.
- Pursue things you're good at and explore things you might be good at.
- Learn from your mistakes.
- Keep an open mind about your own and other people's ideas and don't dwell on what *'might have been.'*
- Learn to sense when your chance for success is good in order to persevere with a project. (In the sporting terminology of the business world - know when you're *'on a roll,'* or learn to tell when it's time to *'take the ball and run with it.'*)

Support groups

Having a support group is essential to maintain positive thinking. Everyone needs someone to support them when they're down and help them celebrate their victories. Think of the people you'd contact if you've had a bad day and needed someone to help you through it or if you've just received exceptionally good news. If you don't have at least two of these people in your life - get them. They're essential for good mental health.

Self-image

There are many other things you can do to improve your self-esteem and self-image. Here are some of them:

1. Write a list of things you like about yourself.
2. Write a list of things you do well. (Read these two lists when your self-esteem is lagging.)

3. Write a list of things you dislike about yourself. How could you change these dislikes to likes?
4. Write a list of things you would like to do better.

The next step is to set some goals to improve your lot in life using the list as a guide. Ask yourself what you're doing to build on your good points. Are you regularly using your unique talents? For example: I've always been an excellent swimmer and I swim whenever I get the chance. For years I had a vague fantasy of becoming a SCUBA diver. As the years passed, the fantasy became more and more fuzzy. One day, after I had written down things I wanted to accomplish in my lifetime, I found that this was one goal I really wanted to achieve. So (rather late in life) I took up SCUBA diving, have spent many happy hours in the briny deep and was one of the minor reasons why I emigrated to Australia. What have *you* been putting off? Don't you think it's about time you did something about it?

How to Dress for Success

How you look, tells others how you feel about yourself. If you dress like a slob, you'll be treated like one. In business it's very important to give the right impression. How to dress in business has been discussed to death, but I'd like to add my two-cents worth. I always advise women to dress the same as women working at a level above them do. For instance - if you're a personal assistant, dress as if you're an executive personal assistant. If you're in line for a supervisory position, dress like a supervisor - even before you obtain the position. It's amazing what a difference this makes to your chances for promotion. If you look the part - you're not as likely to be overlooked. You'll feel much better about yourself as well.

We get so many conflicting pieces of advice on how a woman should dress in business that it can cause a lot of confusion. My suggestion is to dress with femininity and *class*. I don't mean high fashion. That costs too much money and high fashion is often not suitable for office wear. Choose feminine (and I do stress feminine) suits or wear simple dresses that flatter your figure type. Stay clear of wild geometric stripes and flowers. Ruffles are okay as long as they're not of the *'little girl or dance-hall madam'* variety. Use jewellery sparingly and avoid large dangling earrings. Cardigan

159

sweaters signify that you're in a support position, so just wear them at home. Successful business women wear suit jackets if they're cold - not cardigan sweaters! Choose an easy-to-care-for hairstyle and if your hair is long, pin it up. And never chew gum at work!

Next, we'll discuss how to work effectively with male superiors, peers and subordinates.

Chapter Ten

How to work effectively with male superiors, peers and subordinates

Why some men are intimidated by assertive women

How might a man feel when confronted by a woman in what he thinks of as male territory at work? Let's say you're a man working in your backyard (workplace) and you spot a strange animal (a female supervisor) in your yard. This animal isn't like those you normally find in these surroundings (male supervisors). You know you've seen this type of animal in another environment (support position) but don't quite know how it will behave in the present situation. You're rightfully careful. You don't make any moves towards it (ignore the new female supervisor) and merely stand back and study it. If it shows anger or defensiveness towards you, you get ready to defend yourself.

This is the effect a woman has on a man when she enters a male-dominated work environment. The man doesn't know whether the woman is dangerous or not. She seems to be doing things that don't make sense to him and he has a hard time figuring her out. Naturally he's on the defensive! Women in management must try to understand men's inner turmoil and help them adapt by earning their trust and respect. They should not expect immediate acceptance.

To continue with our hypothetical situation, you (the man) are still standing back, studying the animal. You have your defences up, so that you're ready to protect yourself if necessary. When the animal (the woman) makes funny sideways moves towards you (feminine behaviour) you're even more wary.

Now the animal helps itself to some morsel (part of your job) off your patio table. You're naturally annoyed. (This is what some women do - they do part of someone else's job, thinking they're 'helping.') I could go on with this comparison, but I think you get my meaning.

A variety of things may cause men to be intimidated by an assertive woman. Heaven forbid, she may be better than he is! It's almost impossible for some men to visualise themselves reporting to a

161

woman. They think of women supervisors or managers as mother figures - but he's a big boy now! He also might be intimidated by the fact that he doesn't know where women are coming from - they play by a different set of rules.

Many men will interrupt a woman if the conversation isn't going their way or if they think their female supervisor is trying to 'boss them.' If men feel vulnerable, they'll attack or will try to change the course of the conversation. If you're trying to make a point, don't get sidetracked by his diversionary tactics. State that you haven't finished discussing your original topic, then, repeat your original statement to completion.

Colleen was given a senior position, with several men reporting to her. One man objected, because he'd applied for her position. His behaviour bordered on insubordination and Colleen had to deal with it. She said to him privately, *'I know you wanted my position, John and I can relate to how you must feel. I too know what it's like to be overlooked for a promotion, I want and need your co-operation, but I won't tolerate any more negative behaviour from you. Can I count on you to change this?'*

His behaviour improved and he became a good employee. Later Colleen helped John identify why he had not been given her supervisory position. She was able to make sure he obtained the necessary training to equip him for the next promotional opportunity.

Men who feel intimidated by women, often refer to them in derogatory ways, to put them 'in their place.' They say, 'She's pushy,' or 'She's castrating.' He may feel as if you're attacking him, so will defend himself. If you're not aware that you've intimidated him, you'll be shocked when he uses defensive tactics. If this happens, ask yourself what you've done to 'rock the boat' for him. Reassure him that you don't want to invade his turf, but just want and need some space of your own.

How to deal with male chauvinism

There are two forms of male chauvinism. The first kind is blatant. You *know* this man is out to make you feel bad - to keep you in your 'place.' The other is more subtle - and is used by men who often aren't even aware their actions could be classified as chauvinistic.

These are usually older men or men whose upbringing or home situation has conditioned them to think women should be in subservient positions. Many of these men call women 'dear' because women are dear to them. They feel protective towards women and believe it's the man's duty to be the decision-maker and protector.

I once worked with this kind of man. He called me into his office one morning and pointed to an article in our local tabloid that told men not to call their female employees 'dear' or 'honey.' He did this all the time (although he would never have intentionally hurt anyone's feelings) and he was afraid that he might have offended his female staff. I assured him that he had caused no hard feelings, but that he should not use those terms when addressing women. Because this type of chauvinism isn't meant to hurt women, a gentle response to it is advisable. These men normally don't know that what they do or say may be offensive to you. Unless you let them know there's a problem - they're not going to change. Use feedback to give them the opportunity of changing their behaviour.

How should you respond to intentional chauvinism? Men who are blatantly chauvinistic often use very sarcastic comments to get their point across. Realise that when people use the hurting type of sarcasm (which is different from the funny kind comedians use) it's mainly because they want to put others down which in turn makes *them* feel more important. If you respond with sarcasm, - the game only continues. Responding with equal sarcasm or getting angry just plays into their hands - so don't do it!

Analyse why this person feels so inferior that he has to put you down to feel good about himself. Once you have an idea of why this is so, you'll be able to pity him, rather than get upset or angry. Don't react to chauvinism. Turn it off and tune it out. Think to yourself, *'It's too bad this man feels so inadequate he has to put me down to make himself feel more important.'*

If you can't stay quiet or you feel a remark demands a response, try saying: *'Your last comment was very sarcastic and a putdown. Putdowns hurt. Can you explain why you said what you did?'* Or, *'Why did you feel you had to give me a putdown like that?'*

Make him account for his actions. If he is really obnoxious and continues using sarcastic remarks, you might have to resort to this zinger: *'What is it about me that makes you feel so intimidated that*

163

you have to use such cutting, sarcastic remarks?' This one worked for me and it stopped my aggressor cold.

When I was doing research for this book, I interviewed over 700 managers (695 were men) to see why they weren't promoting more women into supervisory or management roles. I was often met by men with crossed arms who used sarcasm during the interview. I learned that I had to change my tactics and start my questions by asking, *'I'm interested in hearing why you think more women are not promoted in your company. Here are some of the reasons that have been related to me by other firms. Do you also find that this is happening here in your company?'* Then I would ask them to think of other reasons they might not promote women.

Sexual Harassment

Research indicates that seventy to eighty percent of women have experienced one or more forms of sexual harassment in the workplace. Even more tragic, is that fifty-two percent have left jobs because of it! This is one work problem that's bothered women for centuries. However, the situation is changing slowly as laws are updated.

Definition

In some areas, sexual harassment can include one or more of the following:

- Unwelcome sexual remarks - i.e.: jokes, innuendoes, teasing, verbal abuse;
- Taunts about a person's body, attire, age, marital status;
- Displays of pornographic, offensive or derogatory pictures;
- Sending dirty jokes via e-mail;
- Practical jokes that cause awkwardness or embarrassment;
- Unwelcome invitations or requests, whether indirect or explicit;
- Intimidation;
- Leering or suggestive gestures;
- Condescension or paternalism that undermines self-respect;
- Unnecessary physical contact - i.e.: touching, patting, pinching, punching or physical assault.

A complaint of sexual harassment does not necessarily mean sexual harassment has actually taken place. An organisation can be held liable for a case of reverse discrimination, when an employee fails to receive merited promotions and bonuses that are granted instead to a co-worker in return for sexual favours given to a manager.

Millie had a problem with her male boss who individually hauled his female employees into his office once or twice a week and bawled them out using profane language. Her local sexual harassment policy states that if others object, men and women in the workplace are not to use words (four-letter or otherwise) that have sexual connotations. This policy applies equally to men and women. If you (a woman) use foul language or tell 'dirty' jokes on the job and other employees (male or female) object to your actions, you can be charged with sexual harassment.

Before men decide to tell a risqué joke they're encouraged to ask themselves how their mother, sister or wife might react. Sexual harassment damages everybody - the victim, the victim's family, the harasser and the company.

How to handle sexual harassment

If you're the object of sexual harassment, take the following steps:

1. Tell the harasser that you object to whatever s/he is doing or saying. Really mean it! If the person doesn't appear to be listening or laughs it off - state that their comments or actions are considered sexual harassment and you expect his or her behaviour to stop immediately. Make sure you document what happened in case it happens again.
2. If the same thing (or something similar) happens again, repeat your earlier objections and back it up with a written letter or e-mail. Relate to your earlier verbal complaints. Make several copies of this letter.
   Keep one copy for your records
   Send one copy to the offending person
   Send one to his or her boss, your boss (and the chief executive officer of your company, if you think it's appropriate).
3. If the behaviour continues or no one steps in to stop the behaviour, lodge a formal complaint with your local equal Rights or Human Rights Commission.

Note:

If the first incident is serious enough, take all three steps at once – object verbally, send a letter (with copies to relevant parties) and lodge a formal complaint with the Human Rights Commission. If a physical assault occurs, call police and take legal steps to charge the person with assault.

One Human Rights Act reads:

'Any person responsible for any act of sexual harassment, any supervisor, manager or person in a position of authority who is aware of the sexual harassment and does not take immediate and appropriate action (as well as the company) will be named in any complaint brought before the Human Rights Commission.'

No longer can others in positions of power 'look the other way' and ignore that sexual harassment is occurring. For instance, if I'm a supervisor and do nothing when I see another person sexually harassing an employee, it's believed that I've condoned the action. If the employee knows that I observed the harassment or know about the situation (and did nothing) s/he can charge both of us with sexual harassment. Co-workers, as well as superiors may be responsible for acts of sexual harassment and can be charged. To obtain information and help with sexual harassment, contact your local Human Rights offices.

There's another form of harassment – workplace bullying. This occurs when a person in a position of power is doing things to make an employee's situation so intolerable that they quit their job. If the employee does leave, in many countries the employee can charge the company with wrongful dismissal and charge the offending party with harassment charges.

If you have been bullied at work, you might like to read my book on this topic: ***Dealing with Workplace bullying – Society's Corporate Disgrace!***

Chapter Eleven

Office and travel tips for
Supervisors and Managers

Rules for female rookies

You've been given that golden opportunity and are now in your first supervisory or management position! Here are some tips that will help you keep climbing the corporate ladder:

1. Climb the ladder one step at a time otherwise you'll miss important training and information.
2. If you've earned a promotion, you should also have received a change in office size and location. Ask to see your new office before accepting the new position. What kind of office did your predecessor have (especially a male one?) Women are usually content with second-rate offices of lowly status. Read up on how status works in an office. Rugs and furniture, the size of the office, whether it has a window and whether it's a corner office - are all important (at least to men) and will identify to others your status in the company.
3. Decorate your office the same way men do. Order the same expensive paintings and plants. Don't bring plants from home - have your company supply them. Make sure your furniture is of the same quality as that in the men's offices.
4. When you obtain a promotion, don't keep looking up to your supervisor for direction - learn to make decisions for each situation based on facts. Learn to research every decision you make.
5. Learn whether someone you now supervise applied for your new job. Call a meeting and ask for his or her co-operation. Explain you'll do everything in your power to make sure s/he is ready for the next promotion that comes along.
6. Learn who to trust and not to trust. Don't make friends before getting the 'lay of the land.' Try talking to the person who was last in your new position. Find out what hidden problems exist that you may have to solve.
7. Try not to make any major changes until you've been on the job for at least two weeks.

167

8. When you start your new job, don't have your boss's personal assistant introduce you to the rest of the staff. Ask your boss to do it; otherwise you'll start off on the wrong foot. The rest of the employees might erroneously believe you're part of the support staff.

9. Don't have recognisably 'female' equipment in your office. This includes files and records (computers and fax machines are okay). Refrain from doing duties that would be classified as 'secretarial' even though it may save you time. If you continue doing clerical tasks, your company will likely object. They're paying you to supervise.

10. Don't use an apologetic attitude when giving work to support staff. They're paid to do that kind of work. You should also have someone specifically appointed to do your work, not just anyone who's available. This support person needs to understand that you have the right to give him or her work and that s/he is responsible for doing the work properly. Their positions should be shown as reporting to you on your departmental organisational chart and both your job descriptions should clearly define the reporting status.

11. Ask your support person to make sure you're put on circulation lists for departmental information that's necessary for making decisions. It's amazing how seldom women get put on these circulation lists (no matter what their rank). This severely limits their knowledge of what's going on in other departments.

12. Order a desk and portable computer and/or tablet. Don't assume you have to supply your own. The status symbol used to be a briefcase; now it's having a mobile phone and portable computer, tablet and iPod.

13. Watch that your office doesn't take on a cluttered look. Get into the habit of clearing your desk at night before you go home.

14. If you're not sure about something, ask a peer (likely male) to explain it to you. Men might not share this information with a male peer (who they see as competitors). Being too proud to admit you don't know something will not make you successful.

15. Order your business cards as soon as you're appointed to the position. The position gets the cards, not the person. The person in charge of ordering cards may not come to you, so you may have to take the initiative. Don't have your home phone number on your cards unless it's absolutely necessary.

16. Join professional organisations that can put you in touch with your peers in different companies.

17. Volunteer for things only if it will help you up the corporate ladder - for instance, to give you more exposure to higher-ups in the company.

18. Never eat at your desk or in the company cafeteria if your peer group eats elsewhere.

19. Company-paid subscriptions to magazines are status symbols - order applicable ones that will help you do your job.

20. Don't become friends with a male misfit. There seems to be one male misfit in every office. This man isn't accepted by his peers for some reason. However, he's very acceptable to the new woman manager, who thinks, *'At least one of my peers has accepted me.'* Men such as this, often make a bee-line for such women out of loneliness. The chances are he's a misfit because he doesn't know the rules himself! Becoming friends with this misfit is tempting, especially by women who find they don't fit in with any set group - the clerical group below them, their male peer group members or their superiors.

21. Attend only those meetings that will be of use to you. If you do attend - be on time! At management meetings, when everyone's eyes rivet on you at coffee break (implying that they expect you to get the coffee) take charge of the situation by saying, *'I take cream and sugar.'*

22. Never be seen with a steno pad (especially at meetings - because you'll be asked to take notes). Send your personal assistant to take notes for you at unimportant meetings. If asked to take minutes at a management meeting, bring your personal assistant to do so, explaining that you can't participate properly when taking notes for others.

23. Accept only positions that will teach you something. If you feel you can adequately perform all the duties of a new position, you were already overqualified the day you started the job. Ask yourself this question every time you're tempted to accept a new position, whether it's a promotion in the same company or one with a new company.

24. Ensure that you receive the same training and educational opportunities as your peer group. Watch for and be open for any on-the-job or off-site training allowed by your company. Those in management positions usually have many opportunities to

obtain further development, so investigate and learn what's available.

25. Most people who are fired or forced to quit, do so not because of incompetence, but because of personal conflicts or office politics, so do your best to get along.

26. Don't allow yourself to be the office scapegoat. Use your assertiveness training. Don't put yourself down.

27. Learn to be a good team player. Quit playing solitaire.

28. Don't act alone. Enlist allies, especially when you're dealing with controversial issues.

29. Don't attempt to hold back vital information merely for your own benefit.

30. Assess your peers' strengths and weaknesses then try to avoid rubbing their noses in the latter. Use their strengths to your and their best advantage.

31. Know your position duties and do them well. Read your job description and ask your supervisor questions to learn what s/he expects from you.

32. If you resign from a position, never burn your bridges by bad-mouthing your former company, boss or workmates. You never know - ten years down the line when there's been a full turnover of staff, just the right job with that company might open up; but you won't be considered, if they check your personnel file and find 'sour grapes.'

33. Learn to control such emotions as anger and fear. Try not to 'lose your cool,' no matter what – and don't be caught crying, which can damage your credibility. It's okay for women to be seen crying in the bedroom (or bathroom) - but not in the boardroom! Men have trouble respecting 'emotional' females. To avoid the sort of frustrating situation that might trigger an overly emotional response (including the impulse to cry) rehearse anticipated bad encounters in advance.

34. Remember that all unsatisfactory situations don't have to be dealt with right away. In many cases you can avoid confrontation for the present, by giving yourself a chance to cool off and return to the situation when you've worked out a suitable strategy.

35. Be willing to express your ideas to your boss, but never criticise or challenge your boss in public. This is a definite no-no. Even if you think your boss is the dumbest, most poorly organised,

most devious person on this earth - don't tell anybody. Keep your opinions to yourself. Remember what your mother used to say: *'If you can't say something nice, say nothing.'* (Sometimes your silence tells it all.)

36. Remember Rule 14 of the Games Played in Business: never date a workmate or a client you deal with on a regular basis. You've probably seen what happens to women who do this. If the male is in a higher position, the woman is the one most likely to leave if the relationship breaks up. Stay clear of anything but platonic relationships with male co-workers and clients.

37. Don't be upset if one of your duties is given to someone else (unless it was because your supervisor felt you were incompetent). This will allow you to go on to bigger and better things.

38. Learn the proper way of accepting compliments for a job well done.

39. If your boss is weak and indecisive, ask for written guidelines relating to areas where you do or do not have the authority to make decisions. Explain that this is to ensure that s/he (the boss) isn't 'bothered' with trivial details. Not only will you be making more decisions but your boss may be glad to toss the responsibility to you. This decision-making can then be added to your job description and later noted on your resume.

40. Don't talk about your highest personal ambitions (especially to male peers). Discuss only your next promotional goal. Choose carefully who you tell about your ambitions, especially if you're the only woman in an otherwise all-male environment. This advice may seem a little ambiguous since I also advised you to let your supervisor know where you want to go career-wise. In this case, I'm speaking about co-workers, not bosses or Human Resources staff. Your male co-workers are likely to think, *'Who does she think she is? She says she's hoping to be the manager of this department eventually. If she thinks she's going to be my boss some day, she's got another think coming.'* They might even sabotage your efforts to climb the ladder. It's still difficult for many men to see themselves reporting to a woman. In fact, for many, it's beyond their comprehension and they'll do everything they can to ensure that it doesn't happen!

41. Whatever your boss thinks is important - make important to you too. You should certainly express your ideas on how something should be done, but if s/he wants a job done a certain way - do it that way. Never dismiss your boss's priorities as being unimportant.

42. Your boss's time is important. Do anything you can to make his or her job run smoothly, but don't hover and get in the way. Be organised and try to anticipate questions your boss may need answered.

43. If you must go to your boss to ask for help in solving a problem, have at least two possible solutions to your problem.

44. Act impeccably. Perform every act as if it were the only thing in the world that mattered.

45. Have a sense of urgency about what you're doing. Don't dawdle or put in time.

46. Plan your time. Think of time as a friend, not an enemy. Don't waste it doing things that are unimportant. Prioritise your work schedule every day.

47. Never reveal all of yourself to other people at work. Hold something in reserve, so that people are never quite sure if they really know you. If you think about it, how much do you know about the private lives of your male bosses and peers?

48. Accept your mistakes and learn from them. Don't repeat mistakes, but don't try to be a perfectionist at everything, either.

49. Don't go after power only for your own personal good. Aim instead to help others along the way. You'll benefit in the end.

50. Develop your own informal lines of communication to learn what's happening in other departments of your company.

51. Don't complain to your supervisor about the behaviour of your peers, unless what they are or aren't doing directly affects how you do your job.

52. Know how your company deals with expense accounts (and don't always go bargain-express.) Use your expense account wisely. Women seem to register at the cheapest hotels they can find and order the cheapest meals they can buy. Don't do this to yourself. Believe me it won't earn you any points and you'll be labelled as 'cheap.' But don't go to the other extreme of using the most expensive hotels and restaurants. There has to be a happy medium. Find out what the majority of your peer group do when they travel and follow their lead.

Tips for Female Travellers

If your company doesn't provide a travel agent - find one and then have your personal assistant make travel arrangements for you. Don't feel you have to do it yourself. Many women still go directly to the airline to buy tickets, but often miss out on special offers from charter airlines or spend hours on-line or on the phone determining this themselves.

If you order airline tickets on-line be sure to check the E-ticket to ensure that the reservation is correct.

Numerous surveys have shown that travel-industry service personnel don't always know how to treat women business travellers. If you travel on business, these tips may help you have a safer, less hectic trip:

1. Make sure you have an up-to-date passport if it's required. Ensure that after you return home there is an extra six months on it before you have to renew it.
2. Get immunisations as required.
3. If you're working in another country, give yourself plenty of time to obtain necessary work permits or visas. Some countries require a visa even if you're not working in that country.
4. When travelling out of the country, make sure you have additional medical coverage. Many credit cards have this coverage if you charge your airfare to the card.
5. Know your blood type in case of emergency.
6. Put identification inside your baggage as well as outside, in case your luggage tag is lost.
7. Pack nylons, belts and other small items inside shoes.
8. Select appropriate luggage. Make sure at least one bag is a carry-on size. Don't pack as if you're going on vacation - just pack one or two (hopefully they don't crease) outfits suitable for the trip. If you find that your clothes are creased when you unpack, ask the hotel to send up an ironing board and iron. If this isn't possible, try hanging them in the bathroom and run the shower on hot until the room fills with steam or try brushing your curling iron or hair dryer (often available in hotel room) over your clothes. (It worked for me!)

9. Always check for damage on a rental car. Do a 'walk-about,' and make sure damage is noted on the contract before taking the vehicle from the lot.

10. Purchase power adapters so that you will be able to use your curling wand or travel iron in the country you're visiting.

11. Keep important documents like traveller's checks and jewellery on your person or in a carry-on bag, purse or briefcase. Leave your expensive jewellery at home. Include a few basic survival items - panty hose, a toilet kit, a change of underwear, etc., in case your bags don't arrive when you do. I learned this lesson on a trip I made to Maui, Hawaii, to conduct seminars. It took my bags twenty-six hours to come the short distance from Oahu to Maui. I had so much carry-on luggage (my seminar material and training films) that I didn't have room to carry a 'survival kit.' Thank goodness my clothes arrived before I had to start instructing or I would have had to purchase a complete outfit (I had travelled in slacks).

12. Allow plenty of time for connecting flights. You might be able to make connections in twenty minutes, but your luggage might not (especially if you're changing planes). Consider retrieving your bags and booking them forward as you go.

13. If you travel with a computer and/or printer, you may have to register your computer and its accessories with customs people at the airport before you leave the country so they don't assume you bought it overseas. And make sure your equipment is compatible with the power source of the country you're visiting. Check to see if you can purchase an adapter that will make it useable in that country. Because most large hotels have business centres, in many cases it's not necessary to take the extra weight and hassle of bringing your own computer equipment. Just bring the files you need on an external hard drive, USB drive, CD or DVD and plug into the hotel's system.

14. Investigate to see if your own car-insurance company offers car rental insurance. Taking extra car insurance from rental firms is very expensive and unnecessary if you can get it through your own insurance agency or credit card.

15. Book into hotels that are advertised as business hotels rather than tourist hotels. You're less likely to get screaming children running up and down the hallways.

16. Make sure your hotel reservation is guaranteed with a payment or credit-card number for the first night. (A confirmed

174

reservation that's not guaranteed will only hold your room until 6:00 pm.)

17. When checking in, let the hotel know you're there on business. Give them your business card. Most hotels have corporate rates.
18. Don't rely solely on the hotel's wake-up call. Carry a small battery operated alarm clock as a backup and use both.
19. Most hotels provide small safes in their hotel rooms. If a room safe is not available, leave valuables in the hotel safe (seldom necessary on business trips, but you may wish to store your passport in a safe if travelling overseas.)
20. Plan to do something at night. Explore the place you're visiting - don't just stay at the hotel. See the sights - go to the theatre or an interesting restaurant. If you're not sure what's happening - ask at the hotel's front desk or concierge.
21. When you travel with male colleagues, don't meet in your hotel room or invite people to have a drink in your room. This eliminates the problem of guests overstaying their welcome and reduces the risk of having to cope with unwanted advances.
22. When the only place you have for a business meeting is your room, ask the hotel to arrange a suite for you. I've had business meetings in rooms that had a table and chairs set up for a business meeting. The room had a hide-a-bed so the bed was out of sight. If your room doesn't appear suitable for a meeting, try a quiet corner of a restaurant or ask the hotel if they have a small meeting room you could use.
23. Don't feel that you should eat only in your room if you're travelling alone. Have a leisurely meal in the dining room and enjoy yourself!
24. When dining - expect a decent table where you have some privacy. Don't accept a table next to a swinging kitchen door! (This is my pet peeve and I quickly ask for a more suitable table.)
25. Your bartender or server should not pass a note to you or serve you an un-requested drink without discussing the situation with you first. If you wish to be alone; tell the bartender.
26. You deserve respect. If you're addressed as 'sweetie' or 'honey' by hotel or restaurant employees - discuss it with the manager.
27. If you're entertaining guests at a restaurant, make it clear to the server (or when you're making the reservation) that the bill is to be charged to your room. It's hard for servers to know where to

place the bill if there are three or four people at a table. Make their job easier.

28. If a late check-out is required; notify the front desk. The porter can keep your luggage in a storage room or possibly they can arrange for you to have the room for an extra couple of hours.

29. At any time, tipping is your choice. However when you travel overseas it's a good idea to check out the tipping rules. If you're uncertain about the country's tipping policies, ask the hotel manager. When receiving services in Canada and the United States, it's customary to tip fifteen percent.

    Tipping is not the general custom in Australia and service charges are not added to accounts by hotels and restaurants. Porters at airports, taxi drivers and hairdressers do not expect to be tipped. At railway terminals, porters have set charges, but not at hotels where you may tip porters for service. In better class restaurants, it's usual to tip food and drink waiters up to 10% of the bill for service

30. If there are too many things that go 'bump' in the night, turn on the air conditioner - the steady hum of the fan will muffle many of the noises. If you have noisy neighbours - complain to the front desk. If you're not satisfied with how they handle this, complain directly to the hotel General Manager.

31. Take pity on the hotel staff. When you've asked room service to bring a meal, an iron, etc., to your room, don't answer the door while improperly dressed (a chronic complaint of room service staff).

Travel Safety Tips

Travelling can be a wonderful experience, but it does have its share **of dangerous situations - especially for the lone female traveller.** Here are some tips that will lower your risk of finding yourself in a difficult situation: Here are some travel safety tips:

- When registering at a hotel, the front desk person may announce the number of your room and give you directions on how to find your room. If this is within hearing distance of others, tell the clerk you'd like another room and explain why. Hotels ought to avoid this practice, which can put a woman's life and belongings in jeopardy. If women complain every time hotels make this mistake, the staff will learn not to do it again.

- If using a porter - have him/her check your room for security. If your room has a balcony - the doors should be secured.
- After your room is made up, hang the 'Do Not Disturb' sign on the door (even when you're not there) to discourage thieves.
- Use your business card on your luggage tags rather than listing your home address. That way, if you're leaving the city, thieves won't be able to tell by looking at your luggage tags, that your home might now be unoccupied.
- When travelling overseas, know whether the water is safe to drink or whether you will require bottled water. If you do, it's wise to pack a bottle in your suitcase, especially if you have a late check-in at the hotel. You may find that the hotel does not supply bottled water.
- If you're arriving late at night, call your hotel and let them know you're on your way. Many have an airport pick-up service.
- In a strange city, take a cab when going out after dark. This eliminates having to walk from a dark parking lot.

Fire Safety

Here are some fire safety tips for travellers:

- When you're settled in your room, determine where the fire escapes are. Identify at least two escape routes, so you have an alternative.
- Count the number of rooms from your suite to the fire escapes and whether they're to the left or right of your room. (If a fire were to occur, you might not be able to see the exit and have to crawl along the floor counting doors to get to safety.)
- Open the exit door to make sure it isn't locked. Determine whether it's an outside fire escape or part of the building itself.
- Look out your room window to notice the height of your room and the nature of your surroundings.
- Notice whether and how windows open. Do they slide right to left, left to right, straight up or don't open at all?
- ***When you retire at night, place your room key on the bedside table within easy reach.***
  If a fire should occur, take the key with you when you leave the room. You may have to return to your room if the smoke is too

heavy or if the fire is too close to your room. If you don't have your key, you may be stranded in a hallway that's an inferno.

- Never use an elevator if there's a fire. The elevator will automatically go to the floor where the fire is situated and will not leave that floor because the buttons are normally heat-sensitive.

Women Travellers' Rooms

Most hotels now provide non-smoking floors and some even provide 'women travellers'' rooms. When booking a room, have your personal assistant ask specifically for a 'woman traveller's' room. Hotels that don't offer this amenity will learn to do so, if enough women ask for it. Rooms provide such welcome amenities as more feminine bedspreads and curtains, fresh flowers and the following extras:

- Skirt hangers (missing in far too many hotels);
- Packages of nail-polish remover (it's against airline regulations to carry bottles of inflammable substances on airplanes);
- Hand and body lotion;
- Shampoo and cream rinse;
- A shower cap;
- A sewing kit;
- Soap for hand laundry;
- A make-up mirror;
- A full-length mirror;
- Full-power plugs near the vanity for hair dryers and curling irons. (I can remember being forced to kneel on the floor of my hotel room using the television as a mirror so I could use the only full-power plug in my room.)

Statistics indicate that more than thirty percent of business travellers are women. This percentage is increasing steadily as women move into higher positions and hotels would be wise to cater to their special needs.

Chapter Twelve

Networking, mentors
and affirmative action

Networking

Networking is the practice of making and using contacts. This is a continual process that goes on in the work world as well as the social circuit. It can be done at seminars, conventions, professional meetings, the neighbourhood community club or on the internet. Friends and acquaintances form a large network, but are not used as contacts often enough by business people.

Rifling through the phone book and making cold calls is now outdated. Networking is far more fun and less threatening. At a networking function, you don't have to pay for a potential client's lunch; s/he's already there waiting for your information.

Many professional organisations encourage members to get together to exchange leads. For example, if a new company has moved into town, there will probably be a need for office furniture, office supplies, recruitment of staff, etc. and network contacts can keep others informed, so they can follow-up and offer their products or services.

Watch how men network. In professional and business groups, business cards are exchanged with an ease that surprises women. To most women, this appears to be a 'hard sell' of the individual and they're reluctant to pass out their cards to just anyone. Men use networking to help each other and the contacts they make in this business-card exchange make it possible. When a man needs a particular kind of expertise, he'll look through his business cards, put a name to a face, remember the impression that person made on him (possibly from notes put on the back of the business card after their initial meeting) and phone the person to set up a meeting.

When a true networker joins a group of people they spend a few seconds deciding whether they should pursue a conversation or move on to another group. If they meet an interesting prospect, they'll spend a few minutes getting acquainted and exchanging business cards. After the meeting, they'd make notes on the back of

179

the card explaining what this person could do for them or what they could do for them and would follow-up at a later date. However, they'd be aware of different cultural customs about this.

For instance, Asian clients are offended if others write on the back of their business cards - so it's important that this isn't done in their presence. There's also a special way of accepting Asian business cards. Asians' business cards are a part of them - and others are expected to accept them with both hands. The receiver of the card would then look at the information on it and make some comment about the Asian's business. But under no conditions would they clasp it with one hand and immediately ram it into their purse or pocket. If they did so, their actions would signify that thought the Asians were unimportant people who would be offended by your show of disrespect.

Most women don't network nearly as well as men. Unfortunately, some don't even have business cards! If your company won't give you business cards - get some made for yourself. Instead of looking elsewhere when they need help, good networkers look through their collection of business cards or check the membership roster of organisations they belong to. They'll probably find the specialist they require listed there. That's what networking is all about. It's people helping people.

If you contact a specialist for advice, it doesn't necessarily mean that the only person you'll help in return is that particular person. Others may call on you for help then pass their own expertise on to someone else. Eventually, the circle will get back to you by someone else helping you (with no obligation in return).

Networkers believe that every new person might be an opportunity to identify a new client or reach new markets. When approaching a new person, start your networking by asking the person what they do. This is the best icebreaker of all. People like to talk about their product or service. They in turn will do the same to you and the networking process is on its way.

As a female underling within a company, when you see that a woman has been promoted in your company – first send her a congratulatory e-mail. Later ask her for lunch (you pay) and discuss what steps she took to get to the position she's in now. This lunch should be initiated about three months after she's had a chance to settle into her position - but send the congratulatory e-mail right away. You can also ask her advice regarding your progress in the company and what she would suggest you do to get ahead.

Anyone who doesn't network will be left behind, so you owe it to yourself to learn how to do it properly. Here are some of the essentials for networking:

- Make as many contacts as possible. Meeting the right people is the key - so be selective about which groups you join.
- Everyone you meet has the potential to help you in business. This could even include Johnny's teacher, whose husband may be in a business that might need your services.
- Don't wait for others to introduce you to new people. Do it yourself; being shy will just hold you back.
- Make sure your contacts know what you do. Make up brochures if necessary or have your business card explain what you do.
- Unless someone is a competitor, never withhold information when you see something you can do for someone (even a person who in all probability will never be able to help you in return). Your help will be remembered and that person could pass on information that may help you in the future.
- Let people know if there have been any changes in what you're doing - such as a new product or service you're offering. Keep up-to-date mailing lists and use them.
- When you get a possible lead - do something about it immediately. Send an e-mail, your brochure or set up a meeting or luncheon to discuss what you can do for the contact. Don't procrastinate!
- When you have the information you need to evaluate a potential client, make sure you don't waste time on clients you can't use. Don't give eighty percent of your time for twenty percent of your business. Concentrate on those clients that will keep giving you continued volume business.
- Use your listening skills when networking. Don't allow yourself to overlook important information about potential clients.

Networks step over hierarchical boundaries and give you access to all levels of management within a company. They enable you to go to the actual decision-maker directly, without the need to work through the intervening layers of people who can't make the decision. Meeting the decision-maker at a conference gives you access to top-level people, ten times faster than the traditional route. Mingling with the right group and joining the right organisations is the necessity for successful networking - not a luxury, as some companies contend.

Every employee should use their network to help keep their company ahead of their competitors. They'd ask contacts to suggest potential clients to them if they didn't need their services or products themselves.

Using the Internet to Network

The internet is one of my most successful networking tools. Because I offer my seminars (and my books are available) almost world-wide, I use its almost free service to keep in touch with clients and potential clients. Instead of having to mail my company brochure to interested clients (which could take up to three weeks to arrive) they can look up my web page and obtain instant information.

I receive e-mail letters from people all over the world wanting more information about my seminars and books, but I also use it myself to expand my client base. For instance, if a client asks me to offer a seminar in Singapore, I contact all my other existing clients in the area (including those in Malaysia, Indonesia and the Philippines) to see if they're interested in having me present seminars for them around the same dates. As well, I'd check with Singapore yellow pages on the internet to identify more possible clients and contact them as well.

This way, I continue to add to my client and potential client base. I also send a monthly company newsletter to interested clients that keep my company's name current in their minds. My website also identifies all the seminars and books I sell and the consulting services I do in the areas of Human Resources and Career Counselling.

How could you be using the internet to expand your knowledge, opportunities or client base?

Mentors

If you talk to successful women, many will tell you that somewhere along the line they had a mentor (for at least part of the time). A mentor is a strong, powerful person who sees raw talent and helps people expand and utilise their unique skills and abilities. They encourage what appear to be ordinary people to achieve success, because they see the hidden talent that these individuals possibly didn't realise they had. The mentor provides information and moral support to help them through good and bad times. Such a person may be an influential senior officer of the employee's company (possibly approaching retirement) but definitely on the lookout to build the company by developing talent among younger employees. It could be a friend of your parents or a best friend who knows the right people.

A mentor is anyone who guides and keeps you from getting into trouble as you progress up the corporate ladder. This person will stop you from making mistakes (that even your male peers make) which will allow you to skip rungs in your promotional climb.

Have you been lucky enough to find a mentor? I've had two in my life. My first mentor was very helpful to me. He was Jim Cebuliak, the president and owner of the Territorial Group of Companies. I admired him, because with little formal training, he had taken a small company and in a short time expanded it into a multi-company empire. I first met him at my job interview and was subsequently hired to set up and head the Human Resources Department for his twelve companies and reported directly to him.

At first I ran into resistance from upper management staff (all male). Understandably, some of the senior executives of his companies balked at the extra work that the implementation of these new personnel procedures caused them. Some had little formal college or university training and objected to the 'newfangled' systems that were being put into place. I reported directly to Jim, so if the managers objected to anything I was doing, they had to complain to him.

He also helped me deal with the more difficult managers and department heads. I learned more about handling difficult people from him than from anyone else in my life. He was highly respected, not only by his management staff, but by his employees as well.

My second mentor materialised when I needed him, but unfortunately I didn't heed his advice. I had more than seven years' experience in human resources - my new boss had only six months. The difficulties in reporting to someone who so clearly lacked the necessary qualifications caused me considerable frustration and eventually, anger.

One day I was having a meeting with a man (who eventually became my mentor) regarding the reclassification of several positions in his department. At the end of the session, he asked me if something was bothering me. I hadn't been aware that my frustration was so obvious. He appeared to be the kind of man who could keep a confidence, so I explained what was happening to me. (Also, I was ready to quit because of the situation - so had nothing to lose by talking about it.)

He listened intently then suggested that I transfer laterally to another department, stay in that department until I was one position higher than my nemesis and then apply for a position in my old department (which would have made me my present boss's boss!) My boss (who was incompetent) was not likely to be promoted higher than his present position.

This man was trying to be my mentor, but I just didn't know what he was talking about! I didn't understand the games played in business. I couldn't see the wisdom in his advice, because I felt I had made human resources my specialty and couldn't see that working in another department would be the way to climb my particular ladder. I blew it - didn't follow his advice and became so discouraged, that I soon left the company.

I didn't understand how wise his counselling was until I started researching for this book and learned about the games played in business. In retrospect, if I had taken his advice, I would probably have become my former boss's boss and have remained with the organisation. As it happened, shortly after that time I started my own business.

Think back. You've probably had someone who has been a mentor and you may not have recognised it. Was there someone in your past that brought out your talents and abilities and helped you 'stretch' your boundaries of knowledge? Is there someone you should be approaching to see if they're willing to help you?

As a woman climbing the corporate ladder, I urge you not to forget to seek that 'raw talent' in other men and women and enjoy the satisfaction of watching them grow. Look for those who have not had the opportunity to use their talents and abilities. Pull them in when you see them headed for trouble. Give constructive criticism and be the first to praise them when they've done a good job.

Unfortunately, male mentors for women are still a rare breed, perhaps because such a relationship is still likely to attract gossip and speculation that sexual 'favours' may be part of the deal. However, if a man is willing to take the chance with his reputation - then the woman should to as well. The pluses far outweigh the minuses, unless there are sexual overtones mixed in with the 'help' received. Women should *never* accept the latter kind of help up the ladder. The help they accept must have no strings attached!

Occasionally there's a negative side to having a mentor. The mentor may take on a protégé for the wrong reasons - out of paternal or maternal feelings or to reinforce his or her own sense of power. Or the protégé may have been looking for a surrogate parent. Often a mentor may dump too many responsibilities and tasks on the protégé, who burns out and rebels, with negative consequences. Accept help from a mentor, but watch that this person doesn't take over your life and make all the decisions for you. Listen to his or her advice, but remember that *you* should judge whether or not you take it.

Occasionally, as a protégé progresses up the ladder, the mentor may become very critical of everything the protégé does. She can't seem to please her mentor no matter what she does. This can be devastating. Can you guess what's happening? The protégé is getting too close and too good - and has become a threat to the mentor. The mentor reacts defensively by making almost impossible demands.

For her own survival, the protégé must wean herself from this type of mentor and it's likely, she no longer needs his or her help anyway. One woman almost destroyed her chances for promotion in a company when this occurred. Her trusted mentor suddenly became very critical and she believed he was right. As an observer, I was able to see what was happening and saved her many months of self-doubt.

185

Fortunately, many mentors remain loyal and good friends even when the protégé reaches the mentor's level. The protégé can now give the mentor peer support - which can be very valuable to them as well.

Affirmative Action

Do you personally believe that affirmative action is a good idea? Have you benefited from affirmative action? Or are you part of the majority who haven't been affected by it? There are pros and cons to affirmative action. The pros, of course, are that companies are forced by the government to hire certain types of employees through a quota system. Without this kind of requirement, many companies would still be hiring predominantly able, white, Anglo-Saxon males. Affirmative-action programs also give members of under-represented groups the opportunity to prove their worth.

There are drawbacks to such programs. Often a woman who has been appointed to a position under an affirmative-action policy finds herself labelled as the department's 'token woman.' The assumption may be that she isn't really qualified for the job; that she's there only because of the quota system. With this kind of attitude to overcome, many women feel they have to prove that they're not only as good as; but better than their male peers. Of course, some fail and the prejudices are reinforced. There's little doubt, however, that voluntary programs do not work.

Women are disadvantaged when:

- Males and females of equal qualifications and experience are appointed at different levels within the same classification;
- Within the same classification or work level, males and females are streamed according to whether the job is more routine or more challenging;
- Males and females of similar educational background are appointed to different classifications, such as clerical and officer, which impedes women's promotional opportunities;
- Males and females are given different degrees of encouragement from their supervisors to attain qualifications, training or experiences necessary for advancement;

186

- Young male employees are perceived as more disadvantaged than their female peers when promotional opportunities are scarce and are given the opportunities when they arise;
- Supervisors positively appraise women who accept their authority and don't assert their right to further advancement;
- Women's prior experiences are not well understood and their relevance to job performance is not considered;
- Women are not benefiting from informal processes which are important for gaining organisational and/or occupational knowledge relevant to advancement;
- Certain kinds of jobs are presented as requiring certain types of qualities or characteristics which are, in fact, not necessary for effective job performance;
- Traditional ways of doing things, traditional conceptions of effective job performance and appropriate job holders, preclude from consideration new and possibly more effective ways of performing in jobs by a range of different people;
- Males in early performance appraisals are given the 'benefit of the doubt' yet positive appraisals for females require a better than average performance;
- Females are not appointed to positions which could be used by males for developmental purposes;
- Organisational rules, such as the requirement for geographic mobility, are applied without regard to the specific circumstances. Women are additionally disadvantaged when such rules are applied more rigidly to them than they are to men in similar circumstances.
- In the area of education for example: the provision of technically-based subjects at a boys' school were not provided at a neighbouring girls' school. This subjected girls to unlawful sex discrimination.

There are no easy answers to the affirmative action problem. Only time will tell whether affirmative action has worked for woman.

Chapter Thirteen

Could I be a successful entrepreneur?

Female Entrepreneurs

The contribution by women to the workforce has grown at more than twice the rate of men over the past 50 years. Women are starting new businesses at double the rate of men and currently own more than 40% of small businesses.

'I have my own business!' Who hasn't wished at one time or another that this statement was true? It's a magical phrase that motivates and challenges many, becomes reality for others, but remains only a dream for most.

Before I re-entered the work force, learned the necessary business practices and gained the self-confidence to go after the carrot (owning my own business) I felt as if I was wasting away. Working for others often left me unsatisfied and I always seemed to *'have the brakes on.'*

However, since I opened my business in May 1982, life has truly begun for me. No more having to do things I felt were unnecessary or redundant. No more red tape. Each and every hour I spend working for my business has a direct bearing on whether my company survives or not. The person who benefits most from my work - is myself. I'm not working, so someone else can reap most of the profit. As a result - my energy level is far greater, I waste less time and put every working minute towards productivity. Mind you, I miss the perks - the coffee and lunch breaks, the paid holidays, the company functions, training opportunities and other frills that large companies offer. I'm also working for the hardest boss I'll ever work for - because my expectations for myself are higher than what most bosses would set for me.

A decade ago, women accounted for only eighteen percent of small businesses. Right now, three times as many women as men are starting small businesses and twice as many women are succeeding. Within the next few years, it's predicted that women will own half of all small businesses. This sharp increase is largely due to the

189

changing economy and the growing number of women entering the labour market.

Women are finding different work in a market in which technology has eliminated many clerical and service positions. They have a greater need for flexible working conditions and their tendency to become impatient with the rules and games of a male-dominated business scene, have encouraged them to look for situations where they can make their own rules.

Incentives and disincentives to self-employment

What motivates most people to become self-employed? Some have been turned off being someone else's employee or by their lack of opportunity to walk through the doors of management. Statistics show that the majority of these self-employed were out of work, felt rejected by their existing employers or felt insecure about their future with their present companies. They were attracted to the idea of having their own business and the independence they visualised they'd have.

They perceived that there would be more rewards for outstanding performance and that they'd be able to go at their own high-energy pace without having to worry about stepping on anyone's toes or intimidating their colleagues and superiors. Some saw a market that wasn't being serviced and went after it. Others came into a sum of money that gave them the opportunity of at least contemplating the idea of being self-employed. Many were just drawn in by the romance of it all.

The following list identifies the most common reasons why men and women want to have their own businesses. They:

- Wish to be independent, be their own boss and make their own decisions.
- See an opportunity for profits - for earning more money.
- Need to work (economic necessity) but can't find what they want in the workplace.
- Want freedom from routine tasks and/or more flexible hours.
- Need to work at home with their families.
- Are looking for personal satisfaction.
- Have identified a market that is not being served.

190

Of course, there are problems to be faced if you decide to go it alone, especially if you're contemplating running a cottage-industry business out of your home. Lack of security is a major one. Can you obtain the necessary financing? What happens if your company goes broke? How about the loneliness you might feel if you work alone out of your home? Will you miss the companionship of workmates at coffee and lunch breaks? How about the missed Christmas parties and company barbecues? Will you be able to work with your children underfoot?

What would happen if you became ill? (Disability insurance bought in advance can help with this one. If there is a professional group you can join, you may be able to get a group rate on premiums, which can be very costly otherwise.) These are all possible negatives.

The successful entrepreneur

Suppose you've decided that the advantages outweigh the disadvantages? Does that mean you're ready to take the plunge? Not quite. First you should ask yourself if you've properly assessed your chances for success. Do you have what it takes to launch a business on your own and make it fly? Do you have the characteristics of a successful entrepreneur? The successful entrepreneur usually:

- Is a good risk taker; not afraid of failure.
- Is not content to be someone's employee (likes recognition, dislikes hierarchies and reporting to a boss or having to justify all new ideas to others before taking action).
- Is more qualified than those s/he reports to.
- Approaches work with as much zest as if it were play.
- Is competitive - expects to win.
- Is good at seeing needs that aren't being met and turning them into business opportunities.
- Is a positive thinker.
- Becomes bored when not challenged.
- Likes starting businesses more than running them (a true entrepreneur).
- Has good organisational abilities.
- Is an avid attendee of seminars.
- Is flexible and open to new ideas.

191

- Has a consistently high energy level.
- Is reluctant to seek outside help (not true with most women).
- Has faith in his or her instincts (or gut reactions).
- Can improvise - does not need to do things *'by the book.'*
- Judges people by their achievements and abilities - rather than their education or pedigree.

Natural entrepreneurs want to call their own shots, love to wheel and deal and don't worry about working around the clock if necessary. They have also:

- Investigated the need for their product or service.
- Evaluated their own preparedness.
- Acquired a basic understanding of the business they're entering.
- Developed a business plan based on market studies.

True entrepreneurs aren't content to leave things as they are. They have considerable confidence in their own ideas and are willing to accept the hard work and long hours they'll expend to make a success of their venture. They recognise that there are bound to be ups and downs in every business venture.

Are you a potential entrepreneur?

Your own character and personality will greatly influence the success of any new business. Here are some things you should ask yourself before you plunge in with both feet:

1. Do you possess the right combination of determination, ambition and self-esteem?
2. Can you cope with the stress of the personal and financial risks you'll be taking when you strike out on your own?
3. Are you patient enough to deal with employees, clients and suppliers?
4. How long will you be expected to work - four hours, eight hours or twelve hours a day? Do you have enough energy to meet these needs?
5. How creative are you? Can you identify needs that no one else sees?
6. Are you a self-starter - or do you need someone else to help *'get your motor running?'*

7. Do you have the time it takes to start a business (ten to twelve hours a day, initially)?
8. If you have family obligations, do you have time to devote to both your family and your business without feeling guilty?
9. If you're married, will your spouse give you the moral support you need to operate a business?
10. Should you maintain your current employment and work part-time at your business or should you jump in with both feet right away. (I found the first alternative better for me. I offered training and development seminars on weekends and in the evenings, years before I started my full-time business).
11. Have you had previous business experience? If not - are you willing to obtain the necessary training, knowledge and skills?
12. Can you and your family survive a financial failure? (The first two years can be very unpredictable.)
13. Are you willing to work *very hard?*
14. Are you able to organise your time (and that of others you may be called upon to supervise)?
15. Do you understand how to lead, motivate and discipline employees? Do you know how to delegate responsibility?
16. Are you good at keeping records or will you have to hire a bookkeeper or accountant?
17. Do you procrastinate or are you able to meet deadlines without problems?
18. Can you make decisions?
19. Are you self-confident?
20. Are you able to persevere?
21. Are you a positive thinker?
22. Do you have a sense of what motivates people to buy?
23. Are you willing to take the risk?

Women as entrepreneurs

Studies comparing the personal characteristics of male and female entrepreneurs have found that female entrepreneurs:

- Are younger than their male counterparts, usually under 39 (men are usually over 50);
- Have several years more education than male entrepreneurs;
- Are significantly less optimistic and less impulsive than their male counterparts;

193

- Are more willing than men to admit when they don't know something;
- Are more inclined than men to use written communication and to read business publications and books;
- Spend anywhere from six to ten months studying the feasibility of a business before committing themselves;
- Start companies that are less profitable in the long run than those started by men because their companies are mainly in the service industry. The big money is in manufacturing and the production of goods, but it's also much riskier financially.

According to a study conducted by Robert D. Hisrich of Boston College and Candida Brush of H. and P. Associates, *'The typical woman entrepreneur is the first born; from at least a middle-class family; has a college degree with a liberal-arts major; is married with children, has a spouse who is supportive and in a professional or technical occupation. She usually works in a traditional women-business area (retail, consulting, personal services); {and} started business because of lack of interest in {available job} areas and job frustration. Her business is usually young and small, with revenues of less than $500,000; and she maintains a controlling interest in the firm.'*

Strengths of female entrepreneurs

Women business owners may appear overly cautious and prudent in their expenditures, but it's their saving grace. They pay themselves realistic salaries and have lower expectations of returns on investment than men. They keep their debt load much lower. It's been determined that this quality - more than any other - is the reason women succeed so well in business. They don't overextend their credit and get in over their heads financially!

Most women are great at bartering. (For example, I've offered seminars in exchange for graphic design work or for accommodation in holiday hotels. I get great graphics for one of my brochures or wonderful holiday accommodation and they obtain top-notch training in return.)

Another advantage some women entrepreneurs have is their ability to type and use word processors. Male entrepreneurs often have to hire people to do the clerical work (or they conscript their wives to do it). Women are more likely to tackle anything that needs doing. They're not too proud to clean out the employees' washroom or vacuum the office when necessary. Men seldom feel comfortable stooping to this level of work.

Many women have their office or work station in their homes, which helps keep overhead low. In my case, several of my male competitors went out of business just as I was starting up. The reason they failed was because their overhead was too high. I continue to conduct my business out of my home, instead of renting an office, do my own computer work and rent training facilities only as I require them.

Female entrepreneurs have the best chance of profiting from a changing economy. Forty-eight percent of new ventures owned by women offer services or information. Twenty-five percent are in the retail sector and only five percent fall into the manufacturing sector. Forty-seven percent of women who start their own business, make it through the first tough years. Male entrepreneurs have a harder time; only twenty-five percent make it through the first three years - mainly because of a too-large a debt load or going too big - too soon.

Women in business are headed in the right direction by offering goods and services to the growing market of working women and two-income families. They're good at defining client needs and often ignore the traditional middle-income mass-market targeted by larger corporations. If they run into roadblocks in obtaining a product or service they feel *should* be available - instead of looking at it as just another frustration - they see it as an opportunity to provide something for themselves and others by opening up a business that provides that service themselves.

Weaknesses of female entrepreneurs

A recent survey showed that three major problems female entrepreneurs have, are in finance, marketing and organisational planning. The most frequent one encountered by women business owners at the start up of their businesses, was difficulty in accessing financing. Over one-third of the women surveyed cited this problem. Almost one-third of the female business owners identified a variety of problems - time management, financial uncertainty, personnel management and establishing credibility.

195

Lack of information and training was cited as the barrier by over nine percent of the business owners, while almost eleven percent of the respondents did not experience any major problems when they were establishing their businesses. Other women identified the unpredictability of the market, the lack of good childcare and problems with morale and self-esteem as being their major difficulties.

Types of self-employment

Suppose you're still undaunted by the drawbacks of self-employment? What kind of business could you start?

Franchises

Another kind of business worth investigating is a franchise. In this case, the parent company supplies guidelines - you're not out there on your own. It is a great testing and learning ground for wary entrepreneurs.

Starting your own or taking over another business

Through experience, you'll learn to avoid mistakes and anticipate problems, plan alternatives and handle crises more efficiently. If you have no experience in the type of business you want to start, work for someone else who is already well established. Pick their brains and learn as much as you can about their business and how they manage it. No amount of experience will replace your own feelings of self-confidence about your ability to succeed in business.

If you're thinking of starting a business you'll need to give it plenty of thought. Read everything you can. Do your homework *before* jumping in. Know the rules about licensing and government regulations.

You'll have to decide whether to be a sole proprietor, go into partnership or incorporate. These are important decisions and before choosing one, you need to learn what each type of company involves. Starting a business with a partner could be compared to getting married and just as hard to get out of. Partners must have compatible goals. It helps if they're complementary, rather than

196

identical in personality, skills and abilities. You and your partner must decide *before* starting your business what might go wrong and work out potential solutions in advance.

Professional Stay-at-homes

Many professional women spend a portion of their day or week working in a formal office setting and the rest working at home. One female lawyer had her company install a computer terminal in her home so she could prepare legal briefs for court in the comfort and quiet of her home (her children were of school age).

The computer age has changed things for many people in such professions as engineering, consulting, software distributing and writing. Personal assistants too, can benefit from this. One woman worked for an engineer and dealt with specifications that were often done in draft form first, then updated and changed several times before its final submission. Many of these *'specs'* took lots of time to prepare. She obtained permission to have a terminal in her home so she could complete these long-term assignments. In addition, she did the company's accounting at home. Her only office appearances were to pick up and deliver assignments and supplies.

Companies that really don't need employees to work in an office setting are realising the advantages of having them work in their homes. Employers save money, because they don't have to provide office space and the administrative overhead that goes with it. If you think your company could benefit from this kind of arrangement - suggest they try it. Outline the savings they'll make if they don't need to supply you with an office. Possibly all you have to do is come in once a week or so to pick up your next batch of work and to drop off completed assignments.

For a home-based worker using a computer, the company will incur the initial expense of hooking up the computer - but from then on, it will save considerable money. Some employers balk at this idea, because they believe home-based workers' productivity will suffer if there's no one around to oversee them. Workers who succeed at working out of their homes tend to be highly independent and have minimal needs for social contacts while working. In fact, such people seem to produce *more* at home - partly because of the lack of interruptions (no children around). If you can choose this route, it's

197

advisable to set up a *real* office and make sure family members know you're not to be disturbed when working - unless there's an emergency.

Part-Time Business

Many self-employed women earn all or a portion of their income by selling door-to-door or by holding home parties. They sell anything from make-up and home cleaners, to house wares. The main attraction of this kind of work is its flexibility. Selling time can be arranged around the needs of the family and the time-wasting commute to and from work is eliminated. There are very few prerequisites - so even those with minimal education can make a go of it. The main requirement for this kind of career is strong motivation and selling ability.

One major disadvantage is that people involved in this kind of work don't receive a regular salary or company benefits. Another disadvantage for some is that it can be difficult to concentrate with children underfoot. Women seem to survive this, though; as one woman said to me: *'I'm so used to doing everything all at once anyway; I know I can handle it!'*

It's important to choose the right product or service to sell. Some women manufacture the products they market. One woman makes custom-made baby quilts for baby showers, flea markets, craft shows, hospital gift shops and small novelty shops and can't keep up with the demand. She has the advantage of working out of her home doing something she enjoys and she is well paid for it! Another woman knits custom-made socks for people who have leg casts and need one huge sock to go over their bare toes. She sells her wares in hospital gift shops and does a booming business.

To be able to sell your product or service properly, you must personally believe that it's better than that of your competitors. Investigate such things as the profit margin, how much you have to invest initially and your anticipated return on investment. How much inventory will you have to keep on hand and can you afford the investment and the financial obligations it might impose? Will you need a car to deliver your product? What will your car expenses be? How about childcare? Will the job pay you enough to reward you for what you put into it?

Although profits may be small initially, you may be able to benefit from tax deductions. For instance, if you use one room in your home to store inventory or conduct business, a portion of mortgage payments or rent can be deducted as a business expense, as can part of your home utility and telephone bills. You can deduct the cost of equipment and other capital expenditures, advertising costs and sometimes even your baby-sitter's salary. If you use your car, your out-of-pocket expenses can be deducted. (However, some tax laws will make it difficult to claim business expenses unless you can *prove* that there really is a business, by pointing to such things as your separate business phone and fax lines, filing cabinets, desks, computers, storage facilities for inventory, etc.)

Ten steps to a successful business

1. Get a marketable idea.
2. Know your product.
3. Get the professional help you need (lawyer, accountant, advice from federal business development agency).
4. Organise your time and work area.
5. Set *realistic* goals.
6. Know your markets and how to reach them.
7. Research your competition.
8. Don't oversell your service or product.
9. Maintain a professional image.
10. Promote your own business.

Know your business

Do you know enough about this particular business to run it successfully? As a business owner, you'll be expected to understand all aspects of your business; pricing, purchasing, financing, accounting, marketing, etc. It's crucial that you recognise your weaknesses and areas of inexperience and either improve those skills through training or make use of appropriate consultants and advisors.

Being your own boss can offer great personal satisfaction, but with it comes the responsibility for making and living with your decisions. The right decision can bring profit and success; the wrong decision can cost you money. Making too many wrong decisions can put you out of business. Be ready!

Marketing

Advance research and preparation is crucial in this area. Is there a market for your product or service? Have you done a market survey to confirm this? Have you chosen *'target markets'* (the most likely groups to buy your product or service?) If you don't know where to start, contact firms that specialise in marketing and have them do the research for you. In the long run, they'll probably do it more cheaply and thoroughly than you can. They'll be able to supply information about such things as:

* Who your competitors are;
* Whether the market you plan to enter is growing or shrinking;
* The general condition of the industry;
* The results of test marketing, using sample groups;
* Your best target markets and names of probable clients;
* How your product or service compares to existing competitive products or services;
* What to charge for your product or service initially and what you could charge eventually as the product or service becomes better known;
* How to break into an existing market or introduce a new product or service;
* The most appropriate media in which to advertise;
* The comparative merits of different types of packaging;
* Your potential market share;
* The best methods of distribution (wholesale, retail, franchise or direct sales);
* Possible international markets.

Distribution

If you can't get a supplier to carry your product - distribute it yourself. The initial costs will be higher, but the control you'll have may be worth it. It may shock you to learn how many intermediaries there are between the point of production and the consumer - and each of these intermediaries is paid a percentage of the retail price. The result is that the initial production price (unit cost) may be only a small fraction of the retail price. If you want to keep your price low, you'll have to eliminate as many of these *'middlemen'* as possible.

200

Pricing

Watch that you don't undersell your competition. Most women undervalue their products or services. Initially, to prove credibility, you might give a lower rate, but eventually you should raise your price to meet that of your competitors. It's ironic, but if you ask a low price, the consumer expects a low-grade product or service even though you may provide a premium product or service. However, if your cost is high, you'd better offer a high-quality product or service.

Distribution

If you can't get a supplier to carry your product - distribute it yourself. The initial costs will be higher, but the control you'll have may be worth it. It may shock you to learn how many intermediaries there are between the point of production and the consumer - and each of these intermediaries is paid a percentage of the retail price. The result is that the initial production price (unit cost) may be only a small fraction of the retail price. If you want to keep your price low, you'll have to eliminate as many of these *'middlemen'* as possible.

Financing

Earlier, I identified financing as one of the biggest problems for women in business. One particular source of difficulty is that some women do not have an independent credit rating. As a result their spouse's signature is required on all financial documents. If a woman in such a situation insists on having her own financing, she'll probably obtain only one-quarter of the amount that would be given to her husband. Women are fighting this battle and many are winning. If you don't have your own credit rating (obtained by having credit cards and bank loans in your own name) start building one now. This will eliminate some of the hassles often experienced by women who wish to borrow money - whether it's for a mortgage or for starting a business.

How much money will you need? This will be determined by your business plan, which we will discuss. Businesses can be started for as little as $500 or they may require an inventory worth $500,000. The variation is considerable. When I started my consulting business, I had low overhead and no inventory. Time was my major investment. I did have a small nest egg, a typewriter, my first computer, a telephone and lots of energy. I've seldom had to borrow money and you may be in the same position.

Make sure you're financially sound before launching into business. You can expect to earn little during the first year or might just keep your head above water. Therefore, you must have a little capital put aside so you don't panic when the going gets tough. For the rest of your financing, bankers or private lenders (family and friends) may be options.

There are two major causes of business failure; poor management and too little money. When you first start a business, it makes good sense to accumulate all the free advice and counsel you can. Many government agencies give free advice to those who take the time to ask. Contact your local Department of Business and Regional Development for this kind of information and pick the brains of successful business owners in your community. Join your local chamber of commerce - get involved and ask questions.

Be prepared to take constructive criticism. Often new entrepreneurs have such a strong commitment to a product, idea or service that they're reluctant to hear any negative comments which could save them considerable time and money.

Business plan

A business plan is a written summary of the overall activities of the business. It shows investors that you've looked thoroughly into the viability of your company. Included in a business plan are:

- Detailed description of the product or service;
- An outline of your marketing strategy;
- A description of your production techniques;
- Information about types of employees you may need to hire;
- The history and present state of the business and the outlook for the future (especially important when you take over a business previously owned by others).

When properly prepared, this plan becomes the blueprint for financing. It has to be complete, well organised and factual. A well-written business plan will be one of the most important elements in your presentation to a banker. It also makes you more organised and aware of pitfalls that may trip you up. A well-written business plan will:

- Make your business more real to you (by forcing you to study the cost-volume-profit relationship that indicate when sales projections have been too optimistic);
- Establish break-even points for you to monitor
- Make you do a complete market survey to establish your potential market and determine your competition;
- Keep you aware of potential danger signals, such as drops in the volume of sales, too much inventory in stock, too much money going out compared to what's coming in;
- Help you identify staffing needs;
- Help you manage and present your company in a professional manner.

Organising

Watch your profitability. This is achieved by establishing various systems to monitor profits - i.e.: bookkeeping, accounting, data-processing, inventory-control systems, etc. Make sure you have adequate insurance coverage, both property and personal.

Many people put off starting a business because they assume they'll have to pay large sums out of their small earnings to such professionals as lawyers and accountants. Investigate before making this assumption. My company was too small to need a full-time accountant, so I had an accountant set up my books and show me how to make entries. Because I have little inventory and there are few transactions, it takes me approximately half an hour per month to do my books. At year-end, I have my accountant do my books and prepare my income-tax forms. Because I now work in so many countries, my accountant looks after any taxes that must be paid. You may not be able to manage with so little paperwork. It depends on the size and type of business you own.

Staffing

You'll be faced with the challenge of finding, interviewing and hiring employees. Be careful not to ask illegal questions in an interview. Managing employees means much more than giving orders. After you hire them, you'll have the task of assigning work, training them and development their talents and motivating them to do their best work.

Managing

Management involves the maximum utilisation of people, money and other resources to achieve the desired result. Poor management is the largest single cause of business failure. Your management skills should be tested *before* your business is established.

Putting your dreams into action

You probably won't succeed without the belief that your product or service is better than that of your competitors. Your next steps are:

1. Prepare your marketing strategy and business plan.
2. Get your money together (or arrange your financing).
3. Choose the best location.
4. Decide upon your business's legal obligations, such as licensing and government regulations.
5. Obtain any necessary business licenses.
6. Set up an accounting system.
7. Determine your pricing schedule.
8. Decide on your advertising strategies (including business cards, brochures and letterhead). Consider advertising on the internet.
9. Hire staff.
10. Prepare for taxes.
11. Open your business!

When you're ready to launch your company, give a press release (free) to your local newspapers. Give them plenty of lead time. If your product or service is unique, try getting on talk shows, especially those that will reach the market you wish to tap. I've found I obtained a far better response from one television talk-show appearance than from thousands of dollars' in newspaper advertising.

Going into business always involves some risk. You can reduce that risk by careful research and thorough advanced planning (put it all in writing). On the whole, women who become entrepreneurs, gain immense satisfaction from what they're doing. For some, the monetary rewards may be less important than the emotional benefits. Others (for the first time they can remember) really feel good about themselves. They've never before felt the kind of *'high'* that comes from this sense of accomplishment. Others enjoy being in control of their destinies for the first time in their lives.

Conclusion

Women who are successful and advance in business keep the following in mind. They:

- Decide where their priorities are - family, career - or both. If it's both, they've learned how to perform the 'balancing act' so they can make it happen.
- Have their home life in order - obtain adequate help at home and hire someone if necessary.
- Have regular family conferences.
- Expect equality with work at home and with childcare.
- Know the nineteen barriers to promotion and work to eliminate as many as possible.
- Have written, realistic career goals.
- Are ready to work overtime, travel on business and re-locate if necessary.
- Do not take excessive time off work either for their own (female problems?) or their children's illnesses.
- Know they can't be super-woman.
- Leave their personal problems at home.
- Evade gossip like the plague.
- Are ready for confrontation with facts, not emotions.
- Constantly build their self-esteem by doing things they do well.
- Continually improve their communication skills.
- Know that if their idea is 'shot down' that they're not a failure and that it's okay to make mistakes - but not the same one twice - to learn from their mistakes.
- Stay away from using 'female tricks.'
- Beware of sabotaging other successful women.
- Have learned how to make independent decisions.
- Know that men often feel the need to 'protect' women from the rat race.
- Know when they're in over their head and ask for training.
- Ask for and expect accurate, up-to-date job descriptions.
- Use their unique talents to the fullest.
- Check their behaviour for 'game playing' - watch they don't try to manipulate others.
- Watch that they don't undermine their boss.

- Make sure they do their job - not someone else's.
- Show respect for their boss.
- Don't jump into promotions without first checking them out.
- Don't accept too many responsibilities.
- Understand company hierarchy, line and staff positions.
- Make sure they have diversified experience.
- Watch for careless work habits.
- Know the supervisory line-of-command.
- Understand military tactics.
- Know team sport's place in the workplace.
- Conform to the rules of the game.
- Use their female strengths.
- Abstain from dating co-workers.
- Know that the boss has the 'right' to take credit for their work but not to do this to their own staff.
- Use logic and facts rather than emotion.
- Know the differences between a job, an occupation and a career.
- Find ways to obtain freedom from pink-collar ghetto positions.
- May face mid-life career changes and are ready for them.
- Know how to determine their transferrable skills.
- Can choose a professional career counsellor and know the tests and tools they'll take to find their ideal careers.
- Have used the goal setting plan.
- Understand the concept of equal pay for work of equal value.
- Comprehend the main disadvantage of being part-time workers.
- Know how to sell themselves on an interview.
- Have learned how to field illegal interview and application form questions.
- Can answer tricky interview questions and overtime requests.
- Feel comfortable asking for a raise.
- Take steps to overcome being overlooked for a promotion.
- Ensure that they're paid adequately when filling acting positions.
- Can handle reporting to female bosses or being one themselves.
- Know how to deal with employee sabotage.
- Discern the importance of obtaining adequate clerical support.
- Can deal with bosses who discipline them in public.

- Know how to remove 'aggressive female' label.
- Will deal with someone who insists on invading their privacy.
- Know the importance of and will ensure that they obtain adequate supervisory training.
- Can deal with the situation where they supervise former peers.
- Comprehend the six behaviour styles and the consequences of using them.
- Know how to deal with manipulators.
- Have confidence in speaking.
- Stay away from self-sabotage, fear of success and failure.
- Can deal with those trying to make them feel guilty.
- Are comfortable taking calculated risks.
- Can accept compliments.
- Know the importance of having a strong support group.
- Are well dressed for business.
- Understand why some men are intimidated by assertive women.
- Are able to work comfortably with an aggressive boss.
- Can handle male chauvinism and sexual harassment.
- Know the rules of female rookies.
- Have learned tips to be successful female travellers and about women travellers' rooms.
- Know and understand fire and safety travel tips.
- Have learned how to network effectively.
- Have found a mentor and are learning how to be one themselves.
- Know the pros and cons of affirmative action.
- Have considered the alternative of being female entrepreneurs.
- Know the incentives and disincentives to self-employment.
- Know whether they have the qualities to be potential entrepreneurs.
- Fathom the strengths and weaknesses of female entrepreneurs.
- Know the alternative types of self-employment.
- Perceive the ten steps to having a successful business.
- Have competency in marketing, pricing, distribution, financing, business plans organising, staffing and managing staff.

And finally, they're ready to put their plan into action to make their dreams become reality. Now that you know how to advance in business and escape the pink-collar ghetto - I have three important final words for you - GO FOR IT!

UNIQUE CAREER COUNSELLING SERVICE

Available via e-mail

Provided by ROBERTA CAVA of:

Cava Consulting,
105 / 3 Township Drive,
Burleigh Heads, Queensland.
4220, Australia.
Ph: 617 5535-0849

In these hard economic times, are you finding it difficult to find suitable employment in your field of work? How would you like to expand those opportunities? This unique career counselling service will enable you to determine your transferrable skills and identify another 20 to 40 occupations where you could use those skills.

An investment of **$175.00** (Aus) will provide you with an extensive report that includes:

- A list of your transferrable skills
- 20 to 30 primary and secondary occupations you could investigate that use your transferrable skills
- A psychological report that includes:

  1. Your strengths in the areas of interest, ability, values, personality, capacity
  2. Interest, ability and personality profiles
  3. What you think your skills are compared to what they really are
  4. Determine your management, persuasive, social artistic, clerical, mechanical, investigative and operational abilities
  5. Whether you are outgoing, reserved, factual, creative, analytical, caring organised or causal
  6. Your ability to think, reason and solve problems
  7. Values inventory
  8. Your stamina level

9. Your I.Q. Score
10. Performance and personality characteristics
11. Motivational and De-motivational factors
12. Whether you have what it takes to become an entrepreneur and have your own business

What will Happen?

After payment is made, you will be able to download a PowerPoint set of questions that you will complete. Some of the questions are timed and every question must be answered.

Your transferrable skills	10 questions
What do you like to do?	7
Timed Test (22 minutes):	30
Likes and Dislikes:	35
What kind of job do you prefer?	40
What kind of person are you?	11
How do you compare with others?	31
Describe your personality	23
Which do you prefer	15
Your preferences	8
Personality Profile	40
Total	**255 questions**

When you have completed the questions, you will e-mail the file to Roberta Cava. She will then do an analysis of your answers and e-mail you a detailed report (approximately 15 pages).

If you're interested in participating in this unique career counselling service, please go to our web page and follow the prompts:

www.dealingwithdifficultpeople.info/unique-career-counselling-service

For more information, contact Roberta Cava at:

rcava@dealingwithdifficultpeople.info

Bibliography

Burne, Eric, *Games People Play – the Psychology of Human Relationships:* Ballantine Books, 1996

Dowling, Colette, *The Cinderella Complex:* New York: Simon and Schuster, 1990

Eichenbaum, Luise and Orbach, Susie, *What Do Women Wan t- Exploding the Myth of Dependency* New York: Berkley Books, 1999

Gilligan, Carol, *In a Different Voice:* Harvard University Press, 1993

Gordon, Dr. Thomas, *Parent Effectiveness Training: The Tested New Way to Raise Responsible Children.* New York: McKay, 1973 and: *Parent Effectiveness Training: Proven Program for Raising Responsible Children,* Three Rivers Press, Nov. 2000

Gray, John**,** *Men are From Mars, Women are from Venus:* Harper Collins, 1998

Harragan, Betty Lehan, *Games Your Mother Never Taught You.* New York: St. Martin's.

La Rouche, Janice , *Strategies for Women at Work.* New York: Avon.

Stechert, Kathryn, *Sweet Success -How to Understand the Men in Your Business Life and Win with Your Own Rules.* New York: Macmillan.

www.ingramcontent.com/pod-product-compliance
Lightning Source LLC
Chambersburg PA
CBHW060552200326
41521CB00007B/555